What We Ought and What We Can

Are we able to do everything we ought to do? According to the important but controversial Ought Implies Can principle, the answer is yes.

In this book Alex King sheds some much-needed light on this principle. She argues that it is flawed because we are obligated to perform some actions that we cannot perform, and goes on to present a suggested theory for anyone who would deny the principle. She examines the traditional motivations for Ought Implies Can, and finds that they to a large degree do not support it. Using examples like gay rights, addiction, and disability, she argues that we can preserve many of the motivations that led us to the principle by thinking more about what we, as individuals or institutions, can fairly demand of ourselves and each other.

Alex King is Assistant Professor of Philosophy at the University at Buffalo, SUNY, USA.

Routledge Focus on Philosophy

Routledge Focus on Philosophy is an exciting and innovative new series, capturing and disseminating some of the best and most exciting new research in philosophy in short book form. Peer reviewed and at a maximum of fifty thousand words shorter than the typical research monograph, *Routledge Focus on Philosophy* titles are available in both ebook and print on demand format. Tackling big topics in a digestible format the series opens up important philosophical research for a wider audience, and as such is invaluable reading for the scholar, researcher and student seeking to keep their finger on the pulse of the discipline. The series also reflects the growing interdisciplinarity within philosophy and will be of interest to those in related disciplines across the humanities and social sciences.

Political Theory and Global Climate Action
Recasting the Public Sphere
Idil Boran

Delusions and Beliefs
A Philosophical Inquiry
Kengo Miyazono

Émilie Du Châtelet and the Foundations of Physical Science
Katherine Brading

Extended Consciousness and Predictive Processing
A Third Wave View
Michael D. Kirchhoff and Julian Kiverstein

What We Ought and What We Can
Alex King

For more information about this series, please visit: www.routledge.com/Routledge-Focus-on-Philosophy/book-series/RFP

What We Ought and What We Can

Alex King

Taylor & Francis Group
LONDON AND NEW YORK

First published 2019 by Routledge
2 Park Square, Milton Park, Abingdon, Oxon OX14 4RN
605 Third Avenue, New York, NY 10017

Routledge is an imprint of the Taylor & Francis Group, an informa business

First issued in paperback 2021

Copyright © 2019 Alex King

The right of Alex King to be identified as author of this work has been asserted by her in accordance with sections 77 and 78 of the Copyright, Designs and Patents Act 1988.

All rights reserved. No part of this book may be reprinted or reproduced or utilised in any form or by any electronic, mechanical, or other means, now known or hereafter invented, including photocopying and recording, or in any information storage or retrieval system, without permission in writing from the publishers.

Notice:
Product or corporate names may be trademarks or registered trademarks, and are used only for identification and explanation without
intent to infringe.

Publisher's Note

The publisher has gone to great lengths to ensure the quality of this reprint but points out that some imperfections in the original copies may be apparent.

British Library Cataloguing-in-Publication Data
A catalogue record for this book is available from the British Library

Library of Congress Cataloging-in-Publication Data
A catalog record for this book has been requested

ISBN: 978-0-8153-6609-6 (hbk)
ISBN: 978-1-03-217826-4 (pbk)
DOI: 10.4324/9781351259958

Typeset in Times New Roman
by Apex CoVantage, LLC

Contents

Acknowledgments   viii

1   The Principle   1
   1. A Common Assumption 1
   2. Ought Implies Can 3
      2.1 What 'Ought' Means 3
      2.2 What 'Implies' Means 7
      2.3 What 'Can' Means 9
      2.4 What the Subjects of the 'Ought' and 'Can' Are 14
      2.5 What the Objects of the 'Ought' and 'Can' Are 14
      2.6 When These Different Things Hold 15
      2.7 Conceptual, Moral, or Metatheoretical? 17
      2.8 The Standard Version 18

2   The Objections   22
   1. General Motivations for Denying OIC 22
      1.1 Sources of Normativity and Ability 22
      1.2 Degrees of Ability 23
      1.3 Normative Parsimony 23
      1.4 Getting Off the Hook Too Easily, or Anti-Pollyannaism 24
   2. Counterexamples and Counterarguments 25
      2.1 Hume's Law and Kant's Law 25
      2.2 Empirical Work on OIC 26
      2.3 Excuses and Justifications 27
      2.4 Promises 27
      2.5 Role Obligations 28

2.6 Moral Dilemmas 29
2.7 Complex Actions 31
2.8 Determinism, Addictions, and Compulsions 33
2.9 The Principle of Alternate Possibilities 34
3. Pragmatic Variations of OIC Rejected 37
3.1 The Presupposition View 37
3.2 The Conversational Implicature View 39
3.3 Pragmatic Views in General 40

3 Must Morality be Fair? 42
1. Motivating Thoughts 42
2. Fairness and Demandingness 42
2.1 Fairness 42
2.2 Demandingness 43
3. Against the Fairness Motivation 45
3.1 Attempt 1: Agential Fairness 46
3.2 Attempt 2: Institutional Fairness 47
3.3 Attempt 3: Fairness as a Substantive Moral Principle 49
3.4 Attempt 4: Fairness as a Pretheoretical Constraint 54

4 Toward a Better Explanation 59
1. Action-Guidingness and Pointlessness 59
2. Against Pointlessness 61
3. Against Action-Guidingness 63
4. Inference to the Best Explanation 66
5. Against the Best Explanation Motivation 67
6. Toward a Better Explanation 68

5 Implications and Applications 78
1. Approach 78
2. Religious Thought 79
3. Determinism, Global and Local 79
3.1 Determinism and Free Will 79
3.2 Physical Disabilities 81
3.3 Addiction and Compulsion 83
4. The law 85

5. Equality and Rights 87
   5.1 Gay Rights 87
   5.2 Affirmative Action 90
6. Ought Implies Feasible 92

6   Conclusion   97

Bibliography   100
Index   107

Acknowledgments

I began thinking about this topic in a graduate seminar on ideal theory in political philosophy, so I suppose that's where the acknowledgments should begin. I am very grateful to Dave Estlund for assigning the Kant essay that set me on this path in the first place, and for encouraging my incipient thoughts on it. He has been a wonderful and kind interlocutor, but always a firm and stalwart defender of Ought Implies Can, and so an extremely useful foil for my thinking on these matters. Before I knew it, I had a dissertation.

Because this book grew out of my dissertation, or more precisely, grew out of issues present in my dissertation, I owe thanks to my friends and mentors in graduate school, who all helped me in various ways. First, I cannot thank enough my adviser, Jamie Dreier, for his support and guidance both then and now. At once my greatest champion and my greatest critic, his encouragement and critical feedback made me the philosopher I am today. I am also very grateful to Nomy Arpaly and Julia Driver who, in addition to Dave Estlund, made up the rest of my dissertation committee. They provided invaluable feedback on the formative stages of what now appears here. I also owe thanks to my dissertation buddy, Steven Yamamoto, and to everyone else throughout graduate school whose comments and discussion helped me think through these matters. I would like to extend particular thanks to Sean Aas, Derek Bowman, Sarah Chervinsky, Emma Cunningham, Phil Galligan, Dana Howard, Charles Larmore, Josh Schechter, and Tim Syme.

Shortly after I arrived at the University at Buffalo (yes, "at"), more commonly known as SUNY Buffalo, I was invited to spend seven months at the Australian National University. I received a research fellowship from the ANU as part of an Australian Research Council (ARC) Discovery Project on Political Normativity and Feasibility Requirements. The project was headed by Nic Southwood and Geoff Brennan, to whom I am very grateful not only for their discussion and friendship (and occasional wine), but for inviting me to spend time at ANU in the first place, where I met many friends and continued refining the ideas contained in this book. Thank you especially to Emily McTernan, whose friendship and feedback – and company during our regular Monday afternoon work sessions – got me through a lot. Thanks also to Christian Barry, Sarah Hannan, Seth Lazar, RJ Leland, Matt Lindauer, Luke Roelofs, and Kai Spiekermann, and all of the usual suspects at ANU tea times and colloquia for innumerable conversations and feedback while I was working through many of these issues.

I am thankful to everyone who along the way enhanced my thinking about these issues with examples, comments on drafts, discussion, and more. Friends and colleagues worth particular mention are Amy Berg, David Braun, Ray Briggs, Mark Budolfson, Norman Dahl, Greg Frost-Arnold, Bob Kelly, Jake Monaghan, Sofia Ortiz, Doug Portmore, Lewis Powell, and Jack Woods.

I have presented various parts of the work that appears here at the Central APA Meeting in 2013, the University of Florida, Texas Christian University, the University at Buffalo, the National University of Singapore, the University of Sydney, the University of Canterbury, the Australian National University, and the Buffalo Women in Philosophy group. I also ran a graduate seminar on OIC in fall 2014. My heartfelt gratitude goes out to all of those audiences. The feedback I received in all of these places was extremely valuable. It helped develop the papers that grew out of those talks, and it helped shape this book.

I also owe special thanks to Jonathan Jenkins Ichikawa, who introduced me to Tony Bruce, my editor at Routledge, and who suggested that I write this book in the first place. I am very grateful to Tony for his encouragement and for his comments on the proposal and manuscript, and to Adam Johnson and Autumn Spalding at Routledge, whose patience with me has not gone unnoticed.

For improvements and feedback on the book itself, I owe most to a set of fantastic referees for Routledge. Their immensely insightful and constructive comments on the proposal and on the manuscript greatly improved the final product. I am genuinely thrilled to have received such a charitable and thoughtful set of referees.

For moral support throughout graduate school and during the past five years, I'd like to thank my dear friends Danielle Sedbrook, Sheena van Leuven, Leslie Widing, and of course my parents, Chris and Marie King.

Finally, I am especially grateful to my partner, Nic Bommarito, whose support and encouragement have been immeasurable, and whose sometimes overly fierce engagement with these topics has always spurred me to better articulate my (and others') views. It's to him that I owe the greatest debt of gratitude. And I really ought to remember this, even in those moments when I can't.

1 The Principle

1. A Common Assumption

A high school student asks her parents which extracurricular group she ought to join. "Well, you ought to join a soup kitchen and give back to the community," one says. "But I can't do that – it's filled up already," she responds. In fact, almost all of them are filled up. The only options left are choir and French club. The parents won't say, "Well, still, you should join the soup kitchen." Instead, they'll select from the options available. In this way, the parents use what their daughter can do as a consideration when determining what she ought to do. Such a decision seems to rely on the assumption that if she really *cannot* join the soup kitchen group, then it isn't true that she *ought to*.

What someone can do is also intertwined with what we think it is appropriate to blame them for or demand that they do. We don't think that a person with quadriplegia ought to stand up and walk over to us. We don't demand that they lift heavy objects or blame them for failing to shake someone's hand. We don't even demand that someone with severe arachnophobia reach out and kill a spider or stroke one's pet tarantula. Moreover, we think that someone who fails to recognize these things is being unfair or cruel. Such a hard person lacks understanding and sympathy for others.

Thoughts along these lines have a long history in philosophy. Pelagius and Aquinas, respectively, write that "nothing impossible has been commanded by the God of justice and majesty,"[1] and that "every sin is voluntary,"[2] and so bring Christian theology in line with the thought that if you really cannot do something, then it isn't true that you ought to. This Pelagian view is also common to non-Christian thinkers who aren't motivated by Biblical quandaries. Immanuel Kant's defense of such a principle is so famous that it has sometimes been known as Kant's Law or Kant's Dictum.[3] Marx, too, in suggesting that we take from each individual according to his ability, suggests that ability enables certain sorts of obligations.[4] Sidgwick writes that "I cannot conceive that I 'ought' to do anything which at the same time I judge that I cannot do."[5] Contemporary philosophers Thomas Nagel and Peter Singer, too, defend this, the former saying that, "'ought' implies 'can', not 'is likely to'"[6] and the latter, that "What is right must be possible."[7]

And it's not only mainstream Western thinkers who have endorsed something along these lines. Mengzi (Mencius) implicitly assumes such a principle when he points out that a king can act compassionately toward his subjects, thereby enabling the corresponding obligations.[8] Sor Juana Inés de la Cruz, alluding to ancient Roman legal theory, writes that "*ad impossibilia nemo tenetur*" or "no one is obliged to do the impossible."[9] Feminist ethical theories, like ethics of care, also defend something like this. Nel Noddings writes of the "I must" feeling at the core of our moral obligations that "I may reject it because I feel that there is nothing I can do."[10] This list is not comprehensive. Many more thinkers have taken for granted an intimate relationship between our abilities and what we ought to do. This is only an assortment.

Let us call the common assumption at the heart of these different views Ought Implies Can, hereafter OIC. That assumption is the topic of this book. In this chapter, I break the principle down into its components and introduce different versions of it, with an eye to highlighting the one that is most commonly defended. The next chapter argues that we should reject OIC in its commonest form, as well as some of its more prominent variations. The third and fourth chapters address the motivations for the principle, and in doing so determine what we give up when we give up OIC. The upshot will be that, in fact, many of the common motivations don't provide support for OIC, but for a collection of other principles, often concerning blameworthiness or the fairness of interpersonal treatment. The end of the fourth chapter argues that OIC is not the best explanation of all of our OIC-regarding intuitions. Instead, I argue, we should think that there are a few different principles at play, and that a full explanation cannot remain neutral about issues in other areas of philosophy, most notably normative ethics. Most crucially, I defend the view that something like OIC is true only for a circumscribed set of oughts and actions, and otherwise it doesn't hold. The fifth chapter looks in more detail at ways in which OIC and OIC-like assumptions are applied or have implications for other debates, with special attention to popular debates in practical ethics. There I use my rival explanation to argue that we don't need to hold on to OIC in order to capture the OIC-like assumptions in these debates. Finally, the concluding chapter contains a brief recap of the dialectic of this book and some closing remarks. The central aims of the book, then, are to provide broad and systematic reasons to reject this extremely pervasive assumption and to outline the sort of view and principles that should replace it.

2. Ought Implies Can

Ought Implies Can (OIC) is a widely held assumption, but we want to know whether it is true. The first step to figuring that out is determining exactly what it means. Notoriously, there are a lot of different things it might mean. Any account of this principle must specify at least six things:

(1) what 'ought' means,
(2) what 'implies' means,
(3) what 'can' means,
(4) what the subjects of the 'ought' and 'can' are,
(5) what the objects of the 'ought' and 'can' are, and
(6) how to temporally index these different elements.

Each of the next six sections will look at these in detail.

It may seem strange that I've only given examples and no explicit statement of the principle so far. There is a reason for this. Different ways of stating the principle often embed answers to these questions. Take, for example:

If someone ought to do something, then they can do it.

This already restricts the way we answer (2), (4), and (5). It assumes that the relevant 'implies' is entailment or something representable by an if-then statement. It assumes that the subjects of the 'ought' and 'can' are individuals, ruling out collectives. And it assumes that objects of 'ought' and 'can' are actions. Although many philosophers are happy to concede all this, it's worth noting that this phrasing simply takes them for granted.

2.1 What 'Ought' Means

We use the English word 'ought' in many different ways. Accordingly, there are many ways to divide this terrain. For example, we use 'ought' for a variety of practical ends: to advise, to prescribe, to assess. But we also use it to indicate the presence of reasons and moral obligations, and to mark all-things-considered rational actions. We use it morally, epistemically, and prudentially; predictively, normatively, and ideally. And this is only a sample of the variety. There is no debate that we *do* use 'ought' in all these ways. The question is: If 'ought' implies 'can', then *which* 'ought' is it?

A couple of points enjoy nearly universal agreement. The 'ought' that implies 'can' cannot be a predictive or ideal ought; rather, it must be normative. Predictive uses of 'ought' occur in sentences like "The mail carrier ought to come by four." But of course this doesn't mean that she can come by four, so the predictive ought does not imply 'can'. A different use that is sometimes difficult to identify is the ideal ought, or more casually, the it-would-be-better-if ought, which appears in sentences like "There ought to be world peace." This certainly isn't a prediction, nor does it suggest that it is anyone's moral duty to bring about world peace. It's just that things would be better if there were world peace. So it is generally agreed that the ideal ought does not imply 'can' either. A normative ought, in the present sense, is an 'ought' used to demand something of someone. We use this 'ought' when we say that you ought to keep a promise you made to a friend, or that you ought to study for a test next week.[11] Though the following uses are more contested, we may think that this is the operative 'ought' when we say that you ought to feel ashamed of yourself, or that you ought to believe what experts say.

Another point that's widely agreed upon has to do with objective and subjective oughts. Doctors ought to prescribe penicillin for many bacterial infections. But some people are allergic to penicillin, and in those cases, doctors can usually find suitable substitutes. Suppose that you are allergic, but neither you nor your doctor know it. There is a sense in which she ought not to prescribe you penicillin (because you're in fact allergic). But there's also a sense in which she ought to prescribe it (because, given her very reasonable beliefs, that's the best option). The former 'ought' is objective; the latter is subjective. Roughly, subjective oughts take into account things like limited knowledge or our own beliefs, while objective oughts don't. OIC is usually taken to apply to only the objective ought.[12] The reason is simple: I may, given my beliefs, think that I ought to do something, and I may also falsely believe that I can do it. In such a case, it seems like I subjectively ought to do something that I cannot actually do. However, we can still say that it's false that I *objectively* ought to do it – perhaps precisely because I cannot actually do it. This is why people tend to defend OIC only for objective ought, though there are some exceptions.[13]

It is here that this nearly universal agreement ends, but there are still some generalizations to be drawn. Let's look at different sorts of considerations that determine whether or not one ought to do something. People who assisted the Underground Railroad in the United States behaved illegally. Yet we readily say that such people did what was morally right. Here, there is a conflict between what people *legally* ought to have done, and what they *morally* ought to have done. It's also plausible that, given enough evidence for something, you *epistemically* ought to believe it. Or, if a sculpture is beautiful, you *aesthetically* ought to appreciate it. And you probably *prudentially* ought to exercise and eat your vegetables. While these particular claims are contestable, they get across an important point: We use 'ought' in different domains, and these different 'oughts' sometimes conflict.

In which of these domains does OIC apply? Some views hold that all genuine (not merely apparent) oughts imply a corresponding 'can'. Such views will notably hold that, if you are very irrational, and you just can't believe a certain thing despite having all the evidence before you, then it just isn't true that you ought to.[14] These extremely inclusive views are in the minority. Philosophers have historically been most concerned with moral uses of 'ought', especially but not exclusively moral uses that indicate the presence of moral obligations, duties, or requirements.[15] A moral ought is most naturally read as suggesting obligation or duty, and this is the way people have tended to present OIC. But moral uses of 'ought' are much more varied than this. Sometimes, when we say that someone ought to do something, we mean there's most reason to do it, and this might go beyond what we are obligated or duty-bound to do, as in cases of supererogation. Others translate the OIC debate into reasons terms. If reasons are the building blocks of oughts, then maybe it is not fundamentally some 'ought', but rather its component reasons that imply 'can'. We might call this view Reasons Imply Can.[16] And such a view has a tidy explanation for OIC: We ought to do things we have some amount of reason to do, or a special kind of reason to do, and because reasons imply 'can', so does 'ought'.

More recent literature has begun to shift focus. We seem to be able to spot OIC at work outside the moral domain. For instance, this book's opening example of the high school student has no special moral component. It's simply about what the student ought to do, very generally speaking. Because of this, views that apply OIC to general practical oughts have become increasingly popular.

Another distinction that is relevant separates *pro tanto* from *ultima facie* oughts.[17] When someone *pro tanto* ought to do something, one really ought to do it. Such an 'ought' may be overridden, but that doesn't make it go away completely. It's possible to describe *pro tanto* oughts in terms of moral reasons or moral obligations. In reasons terms, when someone *pro tanto* ought to do something, one has genuine moral reason to do it. On the second, when one *pro tanto* ought to do something, one has a genuine moral obligation to do it. This obligation may be overridden, but does not thereby lose its obligatoriness or its binding quality. For example, suppose you've promised to meet for lunch at 12:30, but on the way to lunch, you pass by someone who has been in an accident and needs help. Because of your promise, you still ought to meet me at 12:30. But it's also plausible that in this case, you ought to stop and help, and moreover that the latter 'ought' outweighs the former one. Nevertheless, it really is true that you have reason and even are obligated to meet me at 12:30. So, to put it almost too simply, when someone has a *pro tanto* obligation to do something, they are obligated to do it, even if it's overridden.

These two contrast with the *ultima facie* ought, alternately known as ought *sans phrase*, overall ought, or, most commonly, the all-things-considered ought. This 'ought' is by definition never overridden. What we all-things-considered ought to do is what we ought to do after we're done weighing all of the moral considerations.[18] It may be what we're obligated to do or what we have most (moral) reason to do, but in either case, it's what we, at the end of the day, ought to do.

We might deny that obligations can persist while being overridden by other, stronger obligations. If that's so, the distinction between *pro tanto* and all-things-considered oughts collapses. But there's good reason to keep these categories distinct. For example, if I make two conflicting promises, where one is very weighty, while the other is relatively unimportant, it seems that I still do someone a wrong by breaking the lesser promise. In this case, there are two things that I *pro tanto* ought to do (keep each of the promises), but only one thing that I all-things-considered ought to do (keep the weighty promise).

OIC is defended in both forms. Where these distinctions are explicitly addressed, OIC typically invokes the latter,[19] which is often implicitly restricted to the moral domain, but sometimes construed more broadly. However, the many who discuss OIC as a principle concerning moral obligation are most naturally interpreted as defending OIC for *pro tanto* oughts. The idea is that any genuine moral obligation we have, even if overridden, is one that we can fulfill.[20]

To sum up, there are two dominant ways to read the 'ought' in OIC. On the one hand, there is a moral obligation or moral reasons interpretation, which is naturally read as involving a *pro tanto* ought, for the reasons discussed above. On the other, there is the all-things-considered ought, which is usually moral (though is sometimes meant to apply across all domains). In both cases, the 'ought' is normative and is typically objective.

Finally, a quick remark about 'should' and other modal verbs. 'Should' goes relatively undiscussed in the literature, but if discussed is typically taken to be equivalent to 'ought'. There are some nuances ('ought' sounds much stuffier to us now, for example), but the two are effectively the same. 'Must', however, is often thought to be stronger or more binding than 'ought'. "You ought to help" could be a suggestion; "You must help" sounds like a demand. As such, some argue that it's 'must', rather than 'ought', that implies some corresponding 'can'.[21]

2.2 What 'Implies' Means

Regardless of its truth or falsity, we should ask what OIC *is*. Is it a conditional proposition? Is it a rule of inference? If so, what makes it (or would make it) true or valid? If not, then what is it instead?

The literature has suggested two answers that lead to two families of views. On the first, OIC is made true by some entailment (or entailment-like) relationship between the relevant 'ought' and 'can' statements. On the second, OIC functions as a weaker, pragmatic principle. We will look at these in turn.

Many hope that glossing 'implies' as entailment will help clarify the principle, but entailment is also ambiguous. On the one hand, it might mean the sort of relationship that an antecedent bears to its consequent in a conditional statement. But more commonly, entailment is seen as a relationship among sentences or propositions. This gives rise to two further ways of thinking about OIC. According to the first, it is a conditional proposition along the lines of *if one ought, then one can*. The debate is then framed as asking whether this conditional is true, and why. According to the second, the relationship between 'ought' statements and 'can' statements looks more like an inference rule, according to which the following argument is valid:

P1. One ought to do something.
C. One can do it.

The debate would then be framed as asking whether that inference rule is valid, and why.

This distinction has generally been overlooked, and in all honesty, it isn't crucial in most situations. For example, virtually all cases that constitute counterexamples to the conditional proposition also constitute counterexamples to the inference rule, and vice versa. But it is more important if we start thinking about the way the principle functions in a logical system.

There is good reason to prefer the conditional reading. First, it would be odd and maybe ad hoc to populate our logic with an extra inference rule, and moreover one that seems much stronger and more contestable than rules like modus ponens or conjunction elimination. Second, OIC is most plausibly understood, and most frequently defended, as a conceptual or analytic principle, a principle that is true by virtue of the very concepts involved.[22] And although one could defend OIC as an inference rule of certain modal or deontic logics (i.e., the logical systems that govern necessity and possibility or deontic terms like *ought*, *must*, and *can*), it seems that logic itself doesn't make OIC true.[23] Rather, if true, it is true because our very concept of 'ought' involves some sort of 'can'. Analogously, we shouldn't understand the entailment relationship between being a bachelor and being unmarried as a rule of logic, but as a conceptual truth.

So OIC looks best rendered as a conditional that, if true, is true by virtue of the concepts involved. There are, however, alternatives to this worth noting briefly. Maybe OIC is an empirical truth. (This is at least a way of understanding OIC in principle, albeit one that's not defended.) Or maybe OIC is only true as a substantive moral claim, or as a metatheoretical principle. The latter possibilities will occupy more of our discussion below, but it's worth recognizing for now that the truth of OIC will not, in these cases, be analytic.

In the meantime, there are a couple of attractive alternatives for those who find this family of views too strong. These involve weakening the relationship between 'ought' and 'can' to something pragmatic: either presupposition or conversational implicature.

First to the presupposition view.[24] When we talk about things we presuppose in a conversation, we usually mean just the stuff that we assume or take for granted. I assume all kinds of things in virtually all of the conversations that I have: that the gravitational constant won't change, that my father's name is Chris, that 37 is prime, and that my car hasn't been stolen. But, in the technical linguistic sense, I *presuppose* very few of these things in conversations. This technical sense can be brought out in the following sentences:

(1) My cat is on the mat.
(2) I have a cat.

There's something really odd about saying (1) "My cat is on the mat," if I don't have a cat. It feels like the statement somehow doesn't quite make sense. It isn't as straightforwardly evaluable as saying something empirically false or saying something that contradicts an existing belief. Some have tried to capture this oddness by maintaining that, if I don't have a cat, then "My cat is on the mat" lacks a truth-value. This is the semantic (Frege-Strawson) account of presupposition. Others have argued that "My cat is on the mat" is false if I don't have a cat, and attempt to explain the oddness in other ways. This is the fully pragmatic (Russellian) account of presupposition. Either way, if 'ought' presupposes 'can', then the relationship between statements like "She ought to help" and "She can help," is the same as the relationship between statements (1) and (2) above.

The other alternative is to see OIC as an instance of conversational implicature.[25] Take the following scenario. I walk up to you and say, with a desperate look, "My car has run out of gas." You reply, "There's a gas station around the corner." Although you haven't said that the gas station is open, you seem to have communicated to me that it is open. After all, you wouldn't have told me about the gas station if it were defunct. This is conversational implicature. It is one way we communicate things that we don't explicitly say, and it works because when we converse we are trying to communicate with each other. Conversational implicature is a way to do this efficiently.[26] Applying this to OIC, we have the view that when one says "She ought to help," one communicates that she can help without the need to state it explicitly.

To return to our gas scenario for a moment, though, notice that you could instead have replied, "There's a gas station around the corner, but unfortunately it's closed right now." This possibility shows that your statement that there's a gas station around the corner doesn't *entail* that it's open now. Otherwise the second half of your sentence wouldn't make sense. (You can't say things like, "He's a bachelor, but unfortunately he's married.") Similarly, when one says "She ought to help," one communicates that she can help, but one could still meaningfully add, "but unfortunately she can't." In other words, conversational implicature is perfectly compatible with counterexamples to OIC.

These pragmatic alternatives are weaker than entailment views because they allow that it could be true both that someone ought to do something and that she cannot do it. They claim only that it doesn't usually make sense to *say* that someone ought to do something without somehow suggesting that they can do it. As a result, many authors treat pragmatic views as denying OIC. Since in what follows I will reject both entailment and pragmatic accounts, where we stand on this isn't hugely important. What will be important to bear in mind is that there is an important distinction here between conceptual and pragmatic accounts, that the canonical statement of OIC renders it a conceptual or analytic truth, and that the pragmatic versions serve as a deviation from that.

2.3 What 'Can' Means

Of all the components of OIC, 'can' has received the most attention. 'Can' is a wildly flexible word, and it is used in all sorts of ways. Most of these have, at some point, been invoked in discussions of OIC. Here I will discuss different ways to interpret 'can', in rough order from least restrictive to most restrictive. I will start with a reading of 'can' according to which one can do a great many things, and move toward readings of 'can' that increase the limitations on what it makes sense to say that one can do. These give rise to relatively weaker and stronger OIC principles. If, for example, 'can' is relatively inclusive, then the corresponding 'cannot' won't apply as widely, and a corresponding version of OIC will get relatively fewer people out of their 'oughts'. This is what makes the principle a weaker one: It doesn't have much power to get people off the hook. If on the other hand the sense of 'can' is relatively narrow, then the corresponding 'cannot' can be used to get relatively more people out of 'oughts', and thus produce a stronger version of OIC. (Don't worry if this is still a bit confusing. It will become clearer as we go.)

First, we can use it to indicate different varieties of possibility. One option is logical possibility. Something is logically impossible if it is forbidden by logic itself as, for example, contradiction is (in most logics). If the 'can' is logical possibility, then we must look to deontic logic to fully understand OIC.[27] Another option is metaphysical possibility. It's metaphysically possible that humans can run fifty miles an hour – in fact, it may be metaphysically possible for humans to run faster than the speed of light, though this is a matter of debate. A third option is nomological possibility, or something's being possible according to the laws of nature. According to the laws of nature, humans can run fifty miles an hour – in fact, all the way up to the speed of light, but we cannot break it.[28]

Because all three are quite inclusive sorts of possibility, they are less common candidates for the 'can' of OIC.[29] The reason is simple. We want to use OIC to get more people off the hook than these will allow. It's metaphysically possible for me to run fifty miles an hour, but we typically want to use the fact that I cannot run fifty miles an hour to get me off the hook from being morally obligated to do so. So these don't seem like the uses of 'can' we're interested in.

A more common, more restrictive candidate is physical possibility. Though this concept is imprecise and not discussed as commonly in the literature on modality, we have a natural enough understanding of it: I am physically unable to lift something that is 200 lbs. I am also physically able to speak Finnish (the configuration of my throat and mouth is compatible with those sounds), but sparrows are not (the configuration of their throats is not compatible). But physical possibility begins to look less appealing as a way to understand 'can' once we start asking about tougher cases. Is an addict physically able to refrain from a particular instance of addictive behavior? Are you physically able to draw a perfect circle? Am I physically able to comprehend an arbitrarily complex mathematical formula? While there are surely ways of making a notion of physical possibility precise enough to answer these questions (along with some substantive views about the relationship between the mental and the physical), such precision is rare. As a result, these questions often go unanswered. Most importantly, it still looks too inclusive. We typically want, for example, to use the fact that I cannot speak Finnish to get me off the hook from being morally obligated to do so. So physical possibility doesn't seem like the use of 'can' we're interested in, either.

Such questions seem well answered by another common candidate, psychological possibility. Maybe an addict is physically able to avoid addictive behavior, but what is important is that she is psychologically unable to. But again, it's unclear whether I psychologically can speak Finnish. It seems like I can, because even though I don't know how, it's not a matter of some psychological block that I can't. But as we saw, we want to use the fact that I can't speak it to get me off the hook from any corresponding moral obligation. Part of the problem here, as with physical possibility, is that we don't have a precise way of understanding what psychological possibility amount to. Is it what we are able to do, given the facts of our psychological condition? What counts as part of those conditions? It's just terribly unclear. Other, less frequently discussed candidates like circumstantial or practical possibility find themselves in a similar boat. They further restrict the set of possibilities. But if our hope was to get clearer boundaries, these options won't help us much. For example, it is left to context to determine which circumstances are the relevant ones or when an action counts as practically possible. But if we want an analytically true principle to accompany a moral ought, a 'can' on which certain circumstances are sometimes relevant and sometimes not is probably too slippery.[30]

At this point, we won't make progress by further restricting 'can'. Rather, we need a different way to restrict it. By far the most common restriction in contemporary debates about OIC reads 'can' as ability plus opportunity.[31] One way to understand the claim that someone is able to do something is that they have the requisite skills and know-how. This is how we can read the statement, "She is able to pick a lock": she is skilled enough, knows how to do so, has probably done it before, and so on. Someone has the opportunity when they have the requisite resources. She might be able to pick a lock, but if there's no lock around, there is an important sense in which she can't pick one. In other words, if you lack either ability or opportunity, you cannot, in the relevant sense, perform the action. For example, I might be too weak to do push-ups. But I would still have the opportunity to do them unless, say, my hands were tied behind my back. I might be able to scare off a spider, but if there are no spiders around, I don't have the opportunity to do so.

It may be easier to think of one's having the ability and opportunity to do something just in case one would do it (or would tend to do it) if one tried.[32] There are problems with this analysis, but it is a helpfully simple starting point for understanding the view. It's also worth noticing that if you cannot, in this sense, do something, you may still *actually* do it. In other words, inability does not imply *does* not. If you don't have the requisite skills to pick a lock, and therefore lack the ability, you may still luck into success by jiggling the tools around in a lock. It just won't be related to your trying, your control, or your skill.

There are three other considerations to think about when understanding 'can' as ability and opportunity: the knowledge involved, the specific circumstances involved, and human ability in general. First, we typically think that someone's being able to do something implies that they know how to do it. I'm not able to play chess if I don't know the rules, even though my arm can move in the right way and nothing physically prevents me from moving the pieces in accordance with the rules. This comes with hard cases, though. Compare a situation where I am able to bake a cake, but only if I have a recipe to follow, or only if I have assistance from a friend, or only if I take a cooking class. These are difficult gray areas. It's not clear whether I can, in the relevant sense, bake a cake in these three cases. To take the second version, if I really were trying to bake a cake, and I knew my limitations, I would have a friend over to help me. In one way, it might then be true that, if I were to try, I would tend to succeed. On the other hand, there's a straightforward sense in which, if I were to try to bake a cake *right now*, without any friend here to help me, I'd fail, and thus shouldn't count as being able to bake a cake. Cases like these raise some thorny issues, which we'll return to later in the book.[33] For now, it's just worth recognizing that these problems are rooted in the very way that we characterize the 'can' of OIC.

Second, some add a specificity condition, saying that the ability must be *specific* rather than *general*. Although an arachnophobe may generally be able to touch a spider in that she's able to move her arm in a certain way, in the specific situation in which there is a spider in front of her, she is unable to touch it.

The third consideration is related to the second. Not only can we distinguish general and specific abilities within an individual, but we can distinguish general and specific human abilities across individuals, by looking at humans in general versus individual people.[34] If your wrist is broken, you will be unable to lift a weight that a normal human could lift. Though understanding 'can' as involving general human abilities is somewhat plausible at first, it's not obvious how to determine the abilities of humans in general or 'normal humans', and as a result OIC views that rely on this concept are rarely discussed or defended. By-the-numbers approaches generate counterintuitive results, and moreover results that shift over time as certain groups grow more populous than others and technology advances. These and other approaches may also sneak in prejudice. We could end up saying that you ought to lift the weight despite your broken wrist; or if we say that a 'normal human' is sighted, then we have more pernicious conclusions that the blind ought to do many things that they are, as individuals, unable to do.

Although ability plus opportunity is the dominant way to read the 'can' in OIC, there is certainly no consensus on this point. Many other candidates have been suggested. Without going into these in detail, there are some conceptual clusters worth mentioning. Some claim that the relevant 'can' is can be motivated to, can will, or can choose to.[35] Setting aside the potentially confusing recursion, these options are notable for their compatibility with inevitable failure. Someone can be motivated to do something that is *in fact* impossible (in any of the above senses), though this may depend on their not realizing it is impossible. Another family of views ties what we can do to what variously idealized agents would or could do – perhaps rational agents, perhaps virtuous ones. (The 'normal human' view might even be seen as falling into this group.) A third class of views takes what we can do to be what we are likely enough to do or would tend to succeed at, offering perhaps a specific threshold. I cannot hit a bullseye in darts because, although I've done it a few times, I don't do it reliably enough to meet most reasonable thresholds. Similarly, on such a view I cannot win the lottery because there is such a slim chance.[36] In this book, we will focus on the most prominent versions of OIC that are defended, so unfortunately, I cannot address all of these variants in detail. Before closing this section, however, we should look at one final candidate more carefully: 'can' as control.

The 'can' in OIC is sometimes characterized as the control someone has over what they do. This leads to a related principle we'll call *Ought Implies Can Avoid*.[37] If you're genuinely in control of whether you do something, it seems that you not only can do it, but can also avoid doing it. If I can't help but blink, then I'm not really in control of my blinking, even if I do (and therefore can) blink. The principle would be something like this:

Ought Implies Can Avoid (OICA):

If S ought to do something, then S can *not* do it.

Note that the 'can *not*' here should be interpreted in the sense of 'can avoid', 'can refrain', or 'can fail', rather than as 'cannot'. If you cannot breathe, then you're unable to breathe. If you can not breathe, you are able to not breathe by, say, holding your breath. 'Can not' is awkward and potentially confusing, so I am labeling this principle using the word 'avoid', but all of these phrases have slightly different shades of meaning. What's important for us is that interpreting the 'can' of OIC as control means adopting both OIC and OICA.

Interpreting 'can' as control makes OIC look very tightly related to debates about free will, an issue we will return to throughout the book.[38] That said, there is good reason to doubt that OICA, at least, holds in the case of moral obligations. If you cannot fail to fulfill an obligation, so much the better for you! If a teenager promises his parents to stay home one night, and bad weather prevents him from going out, so much the better for his fulfillment of that obligation. We might not *tell* an irrepressibly honest woman she is obligated not to lie, but we could pat her on the back and wax about what a good person she is that she can't even lie, and how lucky she is that no matter what happens, she'll fulfill her obligation not to lie. While OICA is false, it's difficult to deny that something important and related to OIC is going on here. Ideally, an account of our OIC intuitions will also explain what is going on with these cases.[39]

2.4 What the Subjects of the 'Ought' and 'Can' Are

Clarifying the 'ought', 'implies', and 'can' is obviously crucial to articulating OIC. Less obviously, we must also clarify a few other things. It's these other elements that guide the next three sections. A bit of symbolism will help us see the lack of clarity so far. We looked at one way of putting OIC above, namely, *If someone ought to do something, then she can do it.* But this already begs some questions. Better to put it symbolically. Let's put OIC this way for now: *If S ought to A, then S can A*. This section will be concerned with who the subjects of the 'ought' and 'can' are, i.e., the domain of S. The following section will discuss the objects of 'ought' and 'can', i.e., the domain of A.

The domain of S is straightforward. OIC almost always concerns individual agents, since it is agents to whom 'oughts' apply in the first place. We might apply OIC to collectives (companies, institutions, societies, or other groups), but the literature has overwhelmingly set these aside because of the additional complexities they raise.[40]

2.5 What the Objects of the 'Ought' and 'Can' Are

Next, we want to know what sorts of things A ranges over in *If S ought to A, then S can A*. This is more complicated.

If someone ought to believe something, must it be true that they *can* believe it? This principle is, as many have pointed out,[41] pretty implausible. Take a deeply irrational person. Does it fail to be true that they ought to have consistent beliefs? Or that they ought to form beliefs in accordance with their evidence? No – in fact, you might think that what we mean by calling such people irrational is that there is an epistemic standard that they fail to live up to. Admittedly, we are assuming that they cannot help but fail, but that doesn't lessen their irrationality, it just makes it unavoidable. So we should exclude beliefs from the domain of A.

Many have wanted to exclude other sorts of mental states, too. Imagine that a person you intensely dislike does something kind and helpful for you.

It can be true both that you ought to feel grateful and that you can't, given your intense dislike. OIC violations are even clearer in the case of immoral attitudes and emotional reactions. People raised with xenophobic attitudes ought, nevertheless, not to feel disgust, fear, or hatred toward people different from them. But it is sometimes all too true that they can't help but feel this way. Though some defend a strong version of OIC that applies to beliefs and other attitudes, most don't, mainly for the reasons given here.

This leaves actions as the central candidate. Seeing OIC as a principle governing actions is so powerfully dominant that many take it for granted without remark, even writing it into their statements of the principle.[42] Finally, OIC is frequently applied to cases where we should *not* perform an action. Some even define OIC this way, so that we could understand OIC as simply including the following variation: *If S ought not to A, then S can not A.*[43]

2.6 When These Different Things Hold

There is one final piece of information hidden in statements of OIC. Suppose you can't do something *now*, but you can do it later. How does that affect what you ought to do? If you promised to pick me up from the airport next Friday, when exactly is it true that you ought to pick me up? It seems like you're bound by the promise now, all the way until next Friday. But of course you can't pick me up now. I'm not even at the airport! Questions like this give rise to different versions of OIC that have been defended, and about which there is no general consensus.

Again, symbolism will help. OIC says that *If S ought to A, then S can A*. But we need to add some timestamps into this formulation to clarify it. Those timestamps, let's call them *time indexes*, need to answer three questions: (1) At what time is S bound by the 'ought'? (2) When must it be true that S *can* A? And (3) at what time is the action itself supposed to be performed?

We can start by looking at why we might want to separate (1) and (3). Consider the following example. If a friend borrows a book from me and promises to return it when I see her one week from today, she creates an obligation *now*, and thus ought *now*, to return the book *in one week*. This obligation continues to stand over the next seven days. So, tomorrow, she still ought (*then*) to return the book *six days from then*. In other words, she's bound by the 'ought' for an entire week, but she isn't supposed to perform the action of returning the book until one week from today. So we need two different time indexes for the 'ought' and the action. Next, we need to see why we need a third time index for (2), for the time during which it's true that my friend *can* return the book. For now we can assume, although it's somewhat controversial, that she can *now* return the book *in one week*. (The controversy is whether it ever makes sense to say we can perform actions in the future, or whether we can really only perform those actions that we can perform *right now*.)[44] This might just be loose talk, but most defenders of OIC allow room for it. Now suppose that she lost the book on Tuesday, and found it again on Wednesday. In that case, we might want to say that she can't, as of Tuesday night, return the book to me next week, and we might want to ask whether it's still true that she ought to return it to me. The point is just that the time during which it's true that someone can do something might be different from the time during which they ought to, and different yet from the time at which the action itself is supposed to take place.

If we change the above OIC statement to include these three time indexes, we get something like this: If S ought at some time to A at some (potentially different) time, then there is some (possibly third) time at which S can A. Symbolically, we can represent this as

Time-indexed OIC:

$(\forall t_o)(\forall t_a)$(If S ought at t_o to A at t_a, then $[\exists t_c][$S can at t_c A at $t_a])$,

where t_o is the time of the 'ought', t_a is the time of the action, and t_c is the time of the 'can'.[45] The symbolism here can be a little daunting, but it's just the familiar OIC principle with three time indexes added in.[46]

The two major views here diverge on whether to allow the time of the 'ought' and the 'can' (t_o and t_c) to come apart. Let's call views that require that they be simultaneous *synchronic* versions of OIC, and views that allow them to come apart *diachronic* versions. According to synchronic versions, if it's true at one time that someone ought to perform some action, then it must also be true *at that same time* that they can perform that action. Symbolically, it will look like this:

Synchronic OIC:

$(\forall t_o)(\forall t_a)$(If S ought at t_o to A at t_a, then S can at t_o A at t_a).

This is a version of the above time-indexed OIC that holds t_c equal to t_o. According to this view, there is no moment when one ought to do something but cannot. Any flicker in ability causes a corresponding flicker in what one ought to do.[47]

The diachronic version of OIC is less restricted. One loose but intuitive way of putting it is to say that, if someone ought to do something, then they *could have* done it. Because of this, it is sometimes dubbed 'ought implies could have'.[48] Here, there is no restriction saying that the time of the 'ought' and time of the 'can' (t_o and t_c) must be the same, and no restriction that forces them to be different. So it's more accurate, albeit less pithy, to call it 'ought implies can or could have'. Symbolically, we can represent this as

Diachronic OIC:

$(\forall t_o)(\forall t_a)$(If S ought at t_o to A at t_a, then $[\exists t_c][S$ can at t_c A at $t_a])$.

To repeat, there is no general agreement about which of these two we should adopt. There is, however, one infamous reason to prefer the diachronic version. Take the following case: A woman, who's under an obligation to pay back a certain amount of money by Saturday, squanders all her money mid-week. Consequently, she fails to repay the debt on Saturday. This is a case of *culpable inability*, of self-sabotage or self-imposed inability, where someone fails to do what she ought because of prior misbehavior. People tend to think that she does something that she ought not do by failing to repay her debt. But according to synchronic OIC, because she cannot repay the debt *on Saturday*, it's not true that she ought to repay it. But this looks miraculous: She's gotten off the hook by generating her own inability. This is obviously a cost for synchronic OIC, whereas proponents of diachronic OIC can say that, because it's true on Saturday that she *could have* repaid the debt (had she not squandered her money earlier), her inability to repay it on Saturday doesn't get her off the hook.[49]

2.7 Conceptual, Moral, or Metatheoretical?

The views so far have taken OIC as a conceptual or analytic principle, true by virtue of the meanings of 'ought' and 'can'. There are two further ways to understand the principle that deny this feature. One view presents OIC as a first-order moral principle, while the other presents it as a metatheoretical principle concerning moral theories. These are less common than conceptual versions of OIC, but still worth mentioning.

The first option presents OIC as a substantive, first-order moral principle.[50] On this view, OIC has the same status as "You ought not steal." Whether it is true that people ought not steal is something to be decided by a moral theory. It isn't true by virtue of the *meanings* of 'ought' and 'steal' (and 'you' and 'not'). It's the sort of thing about which people might disagree, and their disagreement wouldn't necessarily involve a failure to understand what was being said. In contrast, views on which OIC is a conceptual truth hold that those who dispute OIC are either misunderstanding the concepts involved or else just using different concepts. To explain what OIC would look like as a moral principle, one advocate writes, "one morally ought not to impose, accept, or infer any obligation that cannot be performed by the individual upon whom the obligation is placed."[51] We could render this semi-formally as

Moral OIC:

If S cannot A, then one (morally) ought not demand that S ought to A; or If one is (morally) permitted to demand that S ought to A, then S can A.[52]

The second option is to read OIC as a metatheoretical principle or desideratum governing moral theories.[53] On this view, OIC functions in the way that parsimony or explanatory power functions in building a theory. We use parsimony as a desideratum governing all theorizing, so the idea is to use OIC as a desideratum governing *moral* theorizing. According to parsimony, we should prefer an ontologically simpler theory, other things being equal. Analogously, perhaps we should prefer a moral theory that says people ought to do only the things that they can to one that denies this. On such a view, a moral theory could violate OIC, but this would necessarily come at some theoretical cost.

Though these views will resurface in important ways throughout our discussion, neither is the traditional way to interpret OIC. As such, we will set them aside for the time being.

2.8 *The Standard Version*

We've seen many ways to interpret each of these six elements. These interpretations give rise to a staggering variety of different principles. But putting all these pieces together, dominant versions of OIC emerge:

(1) 'ought': *moral obligation*, or alternatively, *all-(moral)-things-considered 'ought'*,
(2) 'implies': *conceptual or analytic truth*,
(3) 'can': *ability and opportunity*,
(4) subjects of 'ought' and 'can': *individual agents*,
(5) objects of 'ought' and 'can': *actions*,
(6) how to temporally index these different elements: *synchronic* or *diachronic*.

In all but the first and last items, there is a canonical view. To simplify things, I will focus on the moral obligation interpretation of (1) until Chapter 4, and to the extent that I discuss the all-things-considered or reasons interpretations, I will restrict them to the moral domain. I do this for a couple of reasons. Most of the examples that people use involve moral obligations, even if they talk more generally about 'oughts'. I suspect this is at least partly because, in many cases where one is morally obligated to do something, one also all-things-considered ought to do it. Additionally, one doesn't lose much by focusing on these cases, and doing so will help streamline our inquiry. I will also do my best to remain agnostic about (6), the time-indexing issue. For both, however, I will note the places where it becomes important to take a stance. So in what follows, I will treat the following as the standard version of OIC.

Standard OIC:

An agent's being morally obligated to perform some action analytically entails that that agent is able and has the opportunity to perform it.

In the next chapter, we'll look at reasons to doubt this principle.

Notes

1 Rees 1998, 53.
2 Aquinas, *Summa*, II–II, 10, 1, ad. 2.
3 See, e.g., the following passage: "It would not be a duty to aim at a certain effect of our will if this effect were not also possible in experience" (Kant 1996, 280). See also Stern 2004, which contains an important discussion of which version of the principle we should attribute to Kant.
4 Marx 1978, 531.
5 Sidgwick 1981, 33.
6 Nagel 1991, 28, Singer 2004, 28.
7 Nagel 1991, 26.
8 Mencius 2009, 8–9.
9 de la Cruz 2009, 46–47.
10 Noddings 1986, 81.
11 An 'ought' may look normative while being ideal, as in Mark Schroeder's example (2011), "Larry ought to win the lottery." Larry has had a terrible run of luck and we wish for him that he win the lottery, but it's not demanded of Larry that he bring about his winning the lottery. If he tried to do that, we might even take back our wish for his win!
12 Vranas 2007, Graham 2011.
13 E.g., Howard-Snyder 1997, Dorsey 2012. See also Hampshire 1951 for a related, epistemically bounded view.
14 Most famously defended in Alston 1988. See also Bykvist and Hattiangadi 2007, Huss 2009.
15 See, e.g., Widerker 1991, Vranas 2007, Copp 2008, Driver 2011, and Graham 2011.
16 See, e.g., Streumer 2007, 2010, and Vranas 2007.
17 These are also sometimes contrasted with *prima facie* oughts, or merely apparent oughts. OIC is only rarely defended for these because, while it might appear

that one ought to do something, that could turn out to be false precisely because one cannot do it. When defended, it is presented as a constraint on the space of plausible moral *options*: an action is a moral option for someone only if it's something they can (or think they can) do. For the view that *prima facie* 'ought' implies *prima facie* 'can', see Velleman 2000, 93ff.
18 We may also have to weigh the non-moral considerations. What we say here depends on the domain under examination: Is it the moral domain specifically or the much more general practical domain?
19 Stocker 1971, 310, Howard-Snyder 2004, 234, and Graham 2011, 339.
20 For a detailed discussion of pro *tanto* oughts, all-things-considered oughts, and OIC, see Vranas forthcoming.
21 For more, see Kratzer 1977, 1991, McNamara 1996, and von Fintel and Iatridou 2008.
22 See Saka 2000 for a few different readings of the 'implies' of 'ought implies can'. He presents "analytic entailment" as the dominant candidate.
23 See Brown 1977, 207–208 for more on these points.
24 This view began with Hampshire 1951 and Hare 1951, 1963, and its popularity continues. See, e.g., Cooper 1966, Martin 2009, and Besch 2011.
25 This view is most prominently defended by Walter Sinnott-Armstrong 1984, and its popularity continues. See, e.g., Vallentyne 1989, Saka 2000, and Littlejohn 2009.
26 Grice 1967.
27 Sloman 1970.
28 All of this is made even trickier because some hold that metaphysical and nomological possibility are equivalent, while others argue for their distinctness.
29 See Streumer 2007 for an exception.
30 A yet narrower reading of 'can' construes it as moral permissibility. Most think it's trivially true that you are morally permitted to do everything you morally ought to do. Because this yields an extremely weak OIC principle, few have bothered defending it.
31 See, e.g., Vranas 2007, Graham 2011.
32 In fact, this is the traditional conditional analysis of ability, an analysis that arose independently of the OIC debate. Since ability and opportunity as outlined above are *both* captured in this definition, we clearly have two different definitions of ability at play here – one wider, and one narrower. In this book I will stick to the narrower.
33 See Section 2.6, and Section 1.4 in Chapter 2.
34 Hampshire 1951.
35 See, e.g., Harman 1975, Schwan 2017.
36 These are most common in the literature on 'ought' and *feasibility*. See, e.g., Estlund 2011, who talks in terms of being able to "bring oneself to" do something; Lawford-Smith 2013 and Wiens 2016, who both talk in terms of thresholds; and Southwood 2016, who focuses on dispositions to decide, try, and not give up.
37 For example, Ross 1963, 47ff., Kekes 1984, Zimmerman 1996, 26, and even Kant 1998, 54–55 (4:449) defend views of this sort.
38 See Chapter 2, Section 2.8.
39 We'll return to this question in more detail in Chapter 4, Sections 1 and 2, and Chapter 5, Section 3.1.
40 See Lawford-Smith 2013 for an exception.
41 See, e.g., Feldman 2001, Chuard and Southwood 2009, and Mizrahi 2012.

42 See, e.g., Smith 1961, Widerker 1991, Yaffe 1999, Copp 1997, 2003, and Graham 2011.
43 These are especially prevalent in the literature that connects OIC to Frankfurt's Principle of Alternate Possibilities, discussed in the next chapter. Notice too that this principle is different from OICA.
44 We certainly speak as though we can do things in the future. It's completely natural to ask "Can you pick me up in one week?" We don't always have to convert the 'can' to something future-tensed in order for it to make sense: "Will you be able to pick me up in one week?"
45 Some may find it easier to read when put in this equivalent way:

Time-indexed OIC:

$(\forall t_o)(\forall t_a)(\text{If S ought at } t_o \text{ to A at } t_a, \text{ then } [\exists t_c][\text{S can at } t_c \text{ A at } t_a])$.

where t_o is the time of the 'ought', t_a is the time of the action, and t_c is the time of the 'can'.[1] The symbolism here can be a little daunting, but it's just the familiar OIC principle with three time indexes added in.[2]

46 Unfortunately, even the tortured prose formulation along with this complex symbolism does not capture the generality that we would like, since we should really try to accommodate ranges of times. This is easy enough to accomplish, but would require a little more machinery.
47 One might make a further distinction between a *strong synchronic* and a *weak synchronic* OIC. On the strong version, the time of the action is also the time of the 'ought' and 'can'.
48 See, e.g., Sinnott-Armstrong 1984 and 1985 for this term. It is to be distinguished from 'ought to have implies could have', a synchronic view. For the latter, see Zimmerman 1987 and Streumer forthcoming.
49 For an objection to the argument that this counts in favor of diachronic OIC, see King 2019.
50 E.g., Collingridge 1977, Kekes 1984, Forrester 1989, Statman 1995, and Kühler 2012 all endorse some version of this view.
51 Forrester 1989, 31.
52 This is still entailment, and not a different sort of 'implies' at stake. We could instead say that one's being permitted to demand that S ought *conversationally implicates* that S can, although the details of such a principle would be complex to work out.
53 Brown 1977. See Mizrahi 2009 for a discussion of this.

2 The Objections

1. General Motivations for Denying OIC

The literature on OIC is peppered with motivations for adopting OIC. It's said to be necessary for fairness, for morality's action-guidingness, and more. We'll look at these motivations in detail in the following chapters, but first I want to examine motivations for denying OIC. Deniers of OIC most commonly stake their ground on counterexamples to the principle, and sometimes on more general counterarguments. But rarely are we given big picture motivations for rejecting the principle that parallel the motivations for adopting it. Section 1 will remedy this by highlighting major motivations for denying OIC. I present these in the spirit in which motivations for a view are often presented: as *prima facie* support for the view, and as costs to bear by rejecting it. Section 2 will then survey the most prevalent counterexamples and counterarguments, and Section 3 will examine attempts to avoid these problems by weakening OIC to a pragmatic principle.

1.1 Sources of Normativity and Ability

It may be surprising that the first motivation for denying OIC takes us back to Kant, an OIC defender. Kant argues that we know our duty a priori, that is, independently of experience; and that we know what we can do only a posteriori, or through experience. He suggests that, because a priori knowledge is more secure than a posteriori knowledge, we should approach apparent counterexamples to OIC with caution. Beliefs we arrive at a posteriori may be mistaken, so it may turn out that we can actually do something it seemed like we couldn't.[1]

Though Kant uses this to support OIC, we can draw a different lesson from it. The central insight is that normativity (including our reasons and obligations) and our abilities seem to arise in fundamentally distinct ways. One need not adopt Kant's story to have the sense that normativity arises in one way, from one source, and that our abilities arise in a different way, from a potentially quite different source. Whatever views we adopt about the sources of normativity and ability, it would be at least surprising if what we ought to do and what we can do align perfectly, and moreover by virtue of the very concepts involved.

1.2 Degrees of Ability

Deontic concepts like 'ought' and obligation are binary: either you ought to do something or not. Of course, the stringency or seriousness of an 'ought' may come in degrees, but whether you ought to do something does not. On the other hand 'can', especially when understood as ability, does allow degrees. Can I do thirty push-ups? Well, sometimes, if I struggle. Can someone who is very fit and strong? Sure, easily. It's natural to think that even if I am able to do thirty push-ups, someone who has more upper body strength is *more* able. Is a first-year student of Hindi able to speak Hindi? Sort of. Is a native speaker? Definitely.

There is a sense in which ability is binary – the sense in which we go from being unable to do a thing to being able to do it. But in most cases, the path from being unable to being able seems to pass through a sizable gray area, where we're unreliably successful. And even within ability and inability, there is a gradation of greater and lesser ability, and more and less severe inability.

Ultimately, if something morally important needs to be done via the Hindi language, then it makes a moral difference whether you're a first-year Hindi student or a native speaker. Such cases make it look like we want a principle that comes in degrees. The point is not that we want some other principle in addition to OIC. Instead, the very intuitions that support OIC simply do not fit the necessarily binary 'ought'.[2]

1.3 Normative Parsimony

The next motivation tells primarily, though not exclusively, against Standard OIC. It asks us to reflect on the messiness of the discussion of 'ought' in the previous chapter. There, we saw that OIC clearly fails for many oughts: the ideal and predictive, the epistemic, the subjective, as well as 'ought' when applied to beliefs, mental states, and other attitudes. Why think that the moral use of 'ought' when applied to actions is conceptually special?

To approach this from a different angle, recall that the opening high schooler example has no moral element at all. It seems like we should explain example (and others like it) in the same way that we explain the truth of the standard version, which invokes a moral ought. But explanations for why moral oughts imply a corresponding 'can' will apply too narrowly to explain non-moral cases. This tells in favor of broadening OIC to non-domain-specific, all-things-considered oughts. Even in that case, however, it will still be worth wondering why these oughts should entail 'can' when the others mentioned above don't; and why it should be restricted to actions alone, rather than all morally or normatively evaluable states.

1.4 Getting Off the Hook Too Easily, or Anti-Pollyannaism

It's very intuitive that we are sometimes simply unable to do what we ought to do.[3] Someone might say "I know I ought to put my dog to sleep, but I just can't." Religious thought sometimes suggests this, too. The Bible says, "Be ye therefore perfect, even as your Father which is in heaven is perfect,"[4] while maintaining that "all have sinned, and come short of the glory of God."[5] But these thoughts are inconsistent with OIC. OIC entails that, in becoming unable to do something, one's 'ought' disappears. It's worth pausing on this a moment and noticing how counterintuitive this is. The 'ought' just *goes away*. To put it differently, an obligation that one cannot fulfill is no longer an obligation. If our very concepts of 'ought' and 'can' make it impossible for us to be unable to do what we ought to do, then not only must this intuitive thought be false, it must be conceptually confused, and that seems too strong.

As we have seen, a similar thought is sometimes framed as telling against synchronic OIC, in favor of its diachronic counterpart: someone who knowingly makes herself unable to do something thereby makes her obligation disappear. But the present thought is more comprehensive; it's that, regardless of whether anybody is at fault, we sometimes are (or become) unable to do things that we ought to do, and that doesn't seem to make those obligations simply disappear.

Often, too, it seems like we ought to do some things now so that we can do other things in the future. But this, too, is hard to explain without denying OIC. For example, it's clear that a judge who cannot currently make unbiased decisions ought to take steps to decrease her bias. But what explains this? The natural answer is that she ought to make unbiased decisions. But we've already assumed that she can't do that. So OIC not only lets the judge off the hook for making unbiased decisions, but lacks a clear explanation for why she should take steps to decrease her bias. Many things have this structure: learning, improving, and cultivating ourselves, as well as not sabotaging ourselves to preempt obligations that we may see coming down the road. Think, for instance, of someone who doesn't carry cash so that they don't have to give money to any homeless people they see.[6]

All of these suggest a very general motivation for denying OIC, which is that it seems too optimistic of a principle. It gets us off the hook from a lot of things. But why think that we can always do all we ought? Sometimes life is unfair, and we should try to understand that so that we can plan better for the future. As one philosopher puts it, we shouldn't try to adjust morality because the world is unfair; we should try to most closely understand the ways in which problem cases arise so that we can avoid or respond appropriately to them.[7]

2. Counterexamples and Counterarguments

Much more common than motivations for denying OIC are counterarguments and counterexamples to the principle. Let's now look at these in more detail, starting with a historical foray.

2.1 Hume's Law and Kant's Law

Here is David Hume:

> In every system of morality, which I have hitherto met with, I have always remark'd, that the author proceeds for some time in the ordinary way of reasoning, and establishes the being of a God, or makes observations concerning human affairs; when of a sudden I am surpriz'd to find, that instead of the usual copulations of propositions, *is*, and *is not*, I meet with no proposition that is not connected with an *ought*, or an *ought not*. This change is imperceptible; but is, however, of the last consequence. For . . . a reason should be given, for what seems altogether inconceivable, how this new relation can be a deduction from others, which are entirely different from it.[8]

This passage contains what has come to be known as Hume's Law, sometimes also referred to as the is-ought gap. It states that one cannot derive an 'ought' from an 'is', or more generally, moral or normative claims from merely descriptive claims about what the world is like. What exactly Hume meant here is a matter of controversy. Maybe he intended a relatively weak claim about the language of premises and conclusions, or maybe he meant something much stronger about the metaphysical gap between descriptive facts and (alleged) normative facts. Though there is interpretive room for escape, many have seen a tension between Hume's Law and OIC, or Kant's Law.

But what exactly is the tension? It is clear when we look at the contrapositive of OIC, what we might call *Cannot Implies Not-Ought*. If OIC says *if someone ought to do something, then they can do it*, then the contrapositive says that *if someone cannot do something, then it is not true that they ought to do it*.[9] Then the tension is this. Suppose we know that someone cannot do something. This is a descriptive claim, an "observation concerning human affairs." From this, we infer an 'ought' claim, albeit a negative one, namely that it isn't true that they ought to do it.

One might object that this doesn't violate Hume's Law. The claim that one doesn't have an obligation is not an 'ought' claim in the relevant sense. It just says that something *isn't* there. But this can't be right. After all, it is a legal claim to say that we are *not* legally bound to shut off our lights at 10:00 p.m. It doesn't entail that we *do* have any particular legal duty, but it involves, so to speak, looking over all the laws and saying that we don't find any such law there. It therefore makes sense to call this a legal claim, something that we couldn't know without knowing a bunch of things about laws. Similarly, to say that the table is not made of atoms is to make a physical claim, as much as to say that the table is made of atoms. So a negative claim about what obligations we are under *is* a moral claim. Hume's Law can be interpreted as holding that, from the premise that someone cannot do something, we simply cannot infer anything about their obligations. It is that interpretation that generates a conflict with Kant's Law.[10]

It isn't our task to defend Hume's Law, but it is a compelling thesis that many think gets at something deeply true, even if the details aren't always quite right. What is important for us is that holding onto this compelling thesis looks to come at the cost of sacrificing OIC.

2.2 Empirical Work on OIC

There is a small, but growing empirical literature on OIC. This literature investigates what non-philosophers think about different imagined scenarios and whether they take the scenarios to conform to or violate OIC. The attitudes of these non-philosophers, often referred to as "folk intuitions," are then used to inform debate about the principle.

Studies have been rallied to defend both sides of this debate. Some studies present people with a variety of scenarios where an 'ought' exists and then an inability sets in. In one common scenario, for example, someone promises to meet a friend but becomes unable to do so, sometimes even through no fault of their own. Respondents nevertheless agree to the statement that the promisor ought to meet the friend.[11]

Some authors are careful to say that they are not arguing against OIC. They see themselves as presenting evidence that OIC is not the obvious, intuitive, axiomatic principle it is often taken to be. It is something that needs to be defended, rather than taken for granted. In this way, the studies attempt to shift the burden of proof from the OIC denier onto the defender. Others argue that such studies refute OIC.[12] Because, they argue, the entailment is traditionally thought to be conceptual or analytic, the fact that competent thinkers and language users deny it means it's false.

This all looks very good for the OIC denier. Unfortunately, others studies have produced dramatically flipped results where people were very unlikely to deny OIC.[13] So at present there is no consensus in the empirical literature on OIC, and there is still plenty to be explored.

2.3 Excuses and Justifications

Another problem for OIC is to be found in the distinction between justifications and excuses, first presented by J.L. Austin.[14] An action is *justified* when it is what one ought to do. An action is *excused* when it is impermissible, but not suited for full blame. If you have an excuse for missing a meeting, then you should have been there, but because of the circumstances, you deserve less blame than if you missed it simply because you didn't want to go. As Stephen Darwall writes, "If I fail to act as I am morally required *without adequate excuse*, then distinctively second-personal responses like blame and guilt are thereby warranted" (emphasis mine).[15]

So far, OIC is fine. But notice that the fact that one could not have done something is an excuse for not doing it, rather than a justification. This happens if, say, your excuse for missing the meeting is that your car broke down and you couldn't make it. Here we have a case where (1) you do something wrong by missing the meeting (otherwise there would be nothing to excuse), and (2) you could not have avoided missing the meeting. So while the existence of excuses as such is not a problem for OIC, excuses in general open the door to inability-based excuses. And inability-based excuses are a problem.

There are two ways to avoid this conclusion. One might argue that excuses don't entail the wrongness of what was done. You can have an excuse even when what you did was permissible. This denies the initial distinction between justifications and excuses, as some actions will be both excused and justified. One might instead deny that inability ever provides an excuse. How this response fares will turn on the way that we actually use excusing language, perhaps in addition to theories of blame and wrongness. It's thus unclear what independent dialectical power this objection has, though Austin hoped that it would be precisely its independent, undertheorized force that would give it a leg up in the OIC debate.

2.4 Promises

Promises provide an attractive source of counterexamples. Usually a promise to do something simply generates an obligation to do it. In this way, promise-making is a normative power that we have. We can, with a few words, alter the normative landscape. All that is necessary is a speech act with some relatively innocent background conditions. Because promises are such tidy examples of obligation generation, they furnish the most common counterexamples to OIC. Suppose I promise to pick you up at the airport, but I later become unable to. If you haven't released me, I still owe you something – an apology at the very least, or maybe finding a suitable replacement. This moral residue suggests that I have done something wrong, namely, failed to fulfill my promise. My obligation hasn't simply evaporated, despite my inability.

Perhaps a diachronic version of OIC can avoid this. I break my promise because I could have picked you up, even if I can't actually do so when the time comes. But I also seem to violate an obligation if I make that promise, but come to discover that I was *never* actually able to pick you up. (Maybe I make the promise without realizing that my car isn't working.) Even diachronic OIC has difficulty explaining the moral residue here, and on both synchronic and diachronic views it will turn out that I haven't even made a promise in the first place. Cases of this kind are prevalent in the literature: unpayable debts, meetings one cannot make, friends doomed to be stranded at airports.

In response, the OIC defender may take issue with different components of promising as understood here. Maybe promises don't generate obligations, but merely reasons to do something. But why should the case with respect to ability be different when it comes to reasons and obligations, given the very plausible understanding of obligations as equivalent to reasons of sufficient quality or quantity? Maybe, alternatively, promises are inherently conditional, so that "I promise to pick you up" has an implicit "but only if I can." But this account fails to explain the moral residue. My promise simply disappears once I can't fulfill it.

A final consideration in support of promises as counterexamples is this. Promises wouldn't have the force that they seem to if we could just escape them by making ourselves unable to fulfill them, or if they simply went away when we became unable to fulfill them. We could not rely on and derive assurance from promises in the way that we do, if we didn't take them to really bind their promisors to doing what was promised. In a way, it's the very nature of promises that requires they not be so easily gotten rid of.

2.5 Role Obligations

Much like promising, we can voluntarily form obligations by signing contracts: I hereby agree to pay x amount per month for insurance, electricity, or credit debt. I hereby agree not to sue you. Such obligations plausibly follow the model of promising above. But sometimes our obligations outstrip what appears explicitly in the contract. Teachers ought to explain things clearly and lifeguards ought to keep a lookout for swimmers in danger. Furthermore, we can incur obligations like this without entering into a position or role voluntarily. It is a citizen's duty to obey the laws of the land, as it is a father's duty to care for his child. What all these inexplicit obligations have in common is that they derive from the roles we have.[16]

Role obligations pose a problem for OIC because there will very commonly be situations in which a teacher is unable to explain something clearly, a lifeguard's attention lapses, or a citizen cannot obey the law. It's implausible that such obligations come with a but-only-if-you-can clause. Contracts certainly don't. You ought to pay back a debt regardless of whether you can. A teacher who cannot explain the material clearly is failing in an important respect. A father who does not care adequately for his child is not off the hook if he can't.

The best hope for the OIC defender is to say either (1) that contractual and role obligations don't give rise to genuine moral obligations, and that OIC only applies to moral obligations; or (2) that contractual and role obligations don't really exist. But both options deny an impressively vast range of our normative experience, adding further to what we'd have to give up to keep a firm grip on OIC.

2.6 Moral Dilemmas

There is a connection between moral dilemmas and OIC that the previous two sections accentuate. In a moral dilemma, there are two morally required actions that cannot both be performed. For example, we can make promises that turn out to conflict. Suppose that I promise to walk your dog at 5:00, but I have also promised to pick a friend up at the airport when she arrives. It turns out that she is arriving at 5:00, and so I cannot do both. To be more precise, the problem is generated by the following characterization of moral dilemmas.

> **Moral Dilemma:**
>
> A moral dilemma arises when one ought (or is obligated) to A, one ought (or is obligated) to B, and neither is overridden, but one cannot do both A and B.

Such cases look like counterexamples to OIC. You might notice that this still goes a little too quickly. We need a principle that says that when we ought to do A and we ought to do B, that we ought to do A *and* B. This is sometimes called the Agglomeration Principle. We can lay this out a bit more carefully to see exactly what is going on.

(1) One ought to A. (Assumed for Moral Dilemma)
(2) One ought to B. (Assumed for Moral Dilemma)
(3) One ought to A and B. (Agglomeration Principle, from 1 and 2)
(4) If one ought to A and B, then one can A and B. (OIC)
(5) One cannot both A and B. (Assumed for Moral Dilemma)
(6) One ought to A and B, but one cannot A and B. (From 3 and 5)

Here, (4) and (6) form a contradiction. So we have a trilemma, a situation where we must deny at least one of three things: the existence of moral dilemmas, the Agglomeration Principle, or OIC.[17]

First, to the existence of moral dilemmas. Moral dilemmas are usually not thought of as mere conflicts of *pro tanto* oughts. It's plausible that the obligation to pick my friend up on time is more serious than the obligation to walk your dog right at 5:00, and therefore overrides it. In that case, I all-things-considered ought to pick the friend up. While it's true that I break a promise to you, and therefore do something that I *pro tanto* ought not, this is not yet a moral dilemma. However, conflicts of *pro tanto* oughts still present a problem for OIC, since they present situations in which we ought to do two things and cannot do both.

But properly speaking a moral dilemma arises when there are two non-overridden things that one ought to do. But it strikes many as implausible that this could happen. In such a situation, if neither is overridden, many think it's fine to do either, and if one is overridden, there's no dilemma. However, others have attempted to push back on this by presenting cases where it really looks like there are two equally strong, non-overridden obligations.

For example, if the above discussion of promises is right, then we can generate cases where we have two equally serious promises. A potential response is that all such cases involve foreseeably avoidable moral dilemmas, ones that arise only through imperfect planning or reckless promising. But even a perfect planner cannot foresee every circumstance (think of changes in the weather), and anyway dilemmas may arise wholly unrelated to what we voluntarily undertake. It may be that duties to our loved ones and our country sometimes conflict, or our special obligations to family conflict with impersonal demands of justice. Suppose that I ought to spend $50 on music lessons for my nephew, but also ought to donate $50 to an organization that will uphold justice. If I can only do one of these, I am caught in an unavoidable moral dilemma: It was not my choice to have a nephew, nor to be a part of an unjust society, nor to have only $50 to spend in these ways.[18]

The most common response is to deny that one really ought to do both things. Instead, one ought to do the more important thing or, when they're equally important, one ought to do one *or* the other. Replies generally maintain that someone may feel guilt or remorse at not having done one of the two things, and moreover that these feelings would be perfectly justified and rational. And again, there's moral residue, since something seems to be owed to those whose option in the dilemma wasn't chosen. Frankly, it is difficult to adjudicate this debate. Some people are unpersuaded by the cases, though it's worth mentioning that the success of even *one* of these cases is enough to warrant a rejection of OIC. Even if we allow moral dilemmas, however, the defender of OIC may still deny the third thesis of the trilemma: the Agglomeration Principle.

The Agglomeration Principle is a principle of deontic logic, the branch of modal logic that is concerned with deontic concepts like ought and obligation. The principle says that, if one ought to A and one ought to B, then one ought to A and B. For instance, if I ought to exercise and ought to eat well, then I ought to exercise and eat well. But there are reasons to think that this principle is not generally true. If I ought to text you and I ought to drive, then it looks like I ought to text you and drive. But I ought never to text and drive! I suspect that many, perhaps all, counterexamples to the Agglomeration Principle can be resolved in its favor by noticing that the principle isn't committed to saying that one ought to A and B *together* or *simultaneously*. So it's true that I ought to text and drive, but not at the same time.

Even with these responses, the argument against OIC from moral dilemmas is in one way notably weaker than the previous two. More assumptions are needed to generate the problem, none of which is universally accepted. Still, it doesn't essentially rely on promises as ipso facto obligation-generators or on the existence of role obligations, and is in this respect stronger. In any case, it's an undeniably compelling line of thought, and it points to yet another intuitive idea that the OIC defender must give up: either the Agglomeration Principle or the existence of moral dilemmas.[19]

2.7 Complex Actions

Another argument against OIC starts from the admission that OIC is restricted to actions only, with the intent to set aside things like beliefs, character traits, emotions, and other mental states that are frequently involuntary. The worry is that we cannot separate actions out as neatly as this stipulation makes it sound.

Some actions that we are obligated to perform essentially involve certain mental states that we cannot voluntarily bring about. Such actions are not bare, surface behaviors like blinking or moving an arm. They are also more robust than intentional behaviors, like opening doors or putting on clothes. These actions could be called motivated behaviors, behaviors we perform not only intentionally, but accompanied by some further mental state, as when we do something for certain reasons or with a certain motivation. Let's call these *complex actions*, since they involve both a robust mental component as well as a behavioral one. If we ever ought to perform such actions, then there's a problem for OIC. There will be times when we ought to perform such an action but cannot produce the requisite mental state, and therefore cannot perform the action properly speaking (though of course we may be able to perform the associated behavior).

Take, for instance, apologizing. An apology that doesn't express sorrow or regret isn't a real apology. How often is a child rebuked by her parents for crossing her arms and saying sulkily and with a roll of the eyes, "Saw-rry"? Even though she utters the word, and does so intentionally, she clearly doesn't feel sorry for what she's done, and the parents can rightly demand that she *really* apologize. What they mean is not just that she not be sulky and not roll her eyes (though of course they mean that too), but also that she really express sorrow. If she said it sans eye-rolling, but sneakily thought to herself she was really fooling them, she merely pretends to apologize without actually doing so. If her parents found out, they might well continue to be upset with her and explain to her that she still hadn't given a real apology, perhaps trying to convey to her why she had done something worth apologizing for. We can suppose further that she is unable to bring about the feelings appropriate to an apology. She may be too distracted, too angry, or too tired and confused. But then, we have a case where she ought to do something (apologize) and cannot.

This problem is pervasive. Plenty of the things we normally consider actions are best understood as complex actions: we thank, agree, advise, deceive, pretend, focus (along with, e.g., watch and listen as distinct from see and hear), pray, console, insult, and maybe even try, to name a few. While there may be disagreement about the particular members, the list as a whole gives a sense of the kind of actions that pose the problem. When we perform complex actions, we experience a certain mental state (beyond intention) that not only accompanies the action, but partly defines it. Without the relevant mental state, one simply doesn't count as performing the action.

Given the right circumstances, we could be obligated to perform any of these actions. Normal moral discourse undoubtedly supposes that we are generally obligated to perform such actions. There are some very intuitive examples, including apologizing and thanking. The Lutheran Eucharist service includes the words: "We give thanks to you, Lord God Almighty, not as we ought, but as we are able." Catholic doctrine requires confession, and they mean more than simply listing the wrongs one has done. One must feel regret and seek absolution. There may even be other, much more complex actions we ought to perform, like standing by someone, or taking care of them.

One attempt to avoid these counterexamples denies that we have any obligations of this kind. Bearing in mind the cases I've just given, what one ought to do is act thankful, and it's just *separately* true one should feel remorse, perhaps because of a separate obligation, or perhaps because it would decrease moral blame or manifest moral virtue. This response is too hasty.

An obligation to apologize isn't an obligation to say sorry that is supplemented by the obligation to also feel remorse in doing so, or the moral credit we get from being remorseful in doing so. We might actually be obligated to forgo saying sorry rather than say it with no shred of remorse. The complex actions we are obligated to perform cannot always be factored into two parts: an obligation to perform the (intentional) action, and a separate moral claim on the associated mental state – whether it be another obligation or the moral worth or virtue achieved by being in it. Rather, having a certain mental state can bear essentially on how to characterize the morally relevant action we're performing, and thus simply is not distillable into separately evaluable parts. Insofar as we sometimes ought to perform these actions, and sometime are unable to do so, we face counterexamples to OIC.[20]

2.8 Determinism, Addictions, and Compulsions

Many who come to OIC do so through discussions of free will. OIC even sounds like a sort of free will thesis: if we ought to do something, then we're *free* to do it. We can do it, and maybe we can even refrain from doing it (recall 'can' as control from the previous chapter). So it makes sense that there's a tension between accepting determinism and OIC.

Strictly speaking, the two are compatible, but accepting both has extremely counterintuitive implications. If determinism is true, then we cannot do anything other than what we in fact do. If OIC is also true, then we never ought to do anything other than what we in fact do – since after all we can't. In other words, if determinism is true, someone who bullies others can't act more kindly. But if OIC is true, then the fact that the bully can't act more kindly means that it's false that the bully ought to do so. And this is true for *everything* that we don't in fact do. So it's never true that someone who does one thing ought to do another. Everything that we ought to do is not only something we *can* do, but something we *in fact* do. This is incredibly implausible.[21]

One response to this is to accept determinism, but hold onto a form of *compatibilism*, according to which free will and determinism are compatible with each other. Only some forms of compatibilism will work for this purpose. One would have to defend what we might call 'can'-compatibilism, according to which some claims that we can do something other than what we in fact do are compatible with determinism. Strictly speaking, then, because 'can'-compatibilism skirts the question of how to characterize free will, it departs from traditional compatibilist debates. However, this approach requires a careful specification of what 'can' amounts to. As it stands, 'can' involves both ability and opportunity. And whatever we say about the ability to do something we are deterministically not going to do, the *opportunity* to do it seems clearly not to exist. The opportunity to do something, understood as something like external facilitation of the act, is precisely what's missing on a deterministic picture.[22]

Of course, if one is not inclined toward determinism, this problem is no problem at all.[23] But similar worries arise on a different front. Another common counterexample to OIC involves what we might think of as localized determinism: addictions and compulsions.[24] In the previous chapter, we talked about the severe arachnophobe who is unable to reach out and touch a spider. Imagine a kleptomaniac who is similarly psychologically (or even psycho-chemically and thus perhaps physically) compelled to steal. She can't refrain from stealing; she can't *not* steal. But if she cannot refrain, then according to OIC, it's false that she ought to refrain. In other words, OIC implies that it is permissible for her to steal. This also is decidedly implausible. Similarly, an alcoholic who cannot resist taking another drink nevertheless, we think, ought not have another drink. His action is not made permissible once we imagine that he is *so very* addicted that he cannot refrain. But OIC implies, to put it in terms paralleling our determinism discussion, that the alcoholic never ought to perform any other act than the (addictive) act he in fact performs. Such cases make trouble even for those who are fine with giving up determinism.

The strongest response to these cases is to hold either that addictions and compulsions do not typically (or ever) generate inabilities, or that in the rare cases where they are so strong that they do generate inabilities, then it really is false that those people ought to refrain from their addictive or compulsive actions. These responses are significantly weakened once we see that the OIC denier can hold that addictive or compulsive actions can be morally impermissible but not *blameworthy*. (To use the above framework, inability of this kind provides an excuse, rather than a justification.) That way, we can still speak truly when we say that such a person has not done what she ought to have, but be understanding in that we don't hold her morally responsible for it.

2.9 The Principle of Alternate Possibilities

A final objection takes up this last thought. In addition to suggesting that blameworthiness and wrongdoing come apart, the OIC denier may reject

OIC in favor of a slightly different principle that connects moral responsibility to ability. You have to be in control of what you are doing if you are to be morally responsible for it – you have to *choose* to do it. Such a principle has come to be known as the Principle of Alternate Possibilities.

Principle of Alternate Possibilities:

If someone is blameworthy for doing something, then they could have done otherwise.

Many have argued that this is entailed by OIC. But many have also argued that it is itself false, which would be bad news for the OIC defender. If it is false and entailed by OIC, then OIC must be false too. The following argument is one way to represent this alleged entailment.

P1. If S ought not to A, then S can not A. (OIC)
P2. If S is morally blameworthy for A ing, then S ought not A. (Assumption)
C. Therefore, if S is morally blameworthy for A ing, then S can not A. (Principle of Alternate Possibilities)

The first premise is OIC applied to actions we ought *not* do. The second premise claims that a person's being blameworthy for doing something means that they ought not to have done it. This premise creates a conceptual bridge between 'ought' and blameworthiness. And the conclusion looks very much like the Principle of Alternate Possibilities.

Harry Frankfurt famously rejects the Principle of Alternate Possibilities.[25] He argues that there are cases where people do bad things willingly, even though they can't do otherwise. If you don't want to attend a meeting and intentionally stay in your office, you seem to be blameworthy for missing the meeting – and this is true even if your office happened to be locked from the outside for the duration of the meeting. Similarly, if you intentionally make a cruel joke, you are blameworthy for it, *even if* an evil genius has implanted a chip in your brain that would have kicked in and forced you to make the cruel joke had you not yourself chosen to do so. In such situations, sometimes called *Frankfurt cases*, you are morally blameworthy despite being unable to do otherwise. If we are convinced by such cases, as many have been, it looks like there is a problem for OIC.

According to the above argument, denying the Principle of Alternate Possibilities entails denying OIC, and what's more, we can use that argument to transform Frankfurt's own counterexamples to the Principle of Alternate Possibilities into counterexamples to OIC. Observe: If you intentionally make a cruel joke, you are blameworthy for it, even if (as is true in the situation above) you could not have done otherwise (because of the chip). But if you are blameworthy for making that cruel joke, then you have done something wrong, i.e., something you ought not to have done. Thus, you have done something you ought not to have done, *despite* its also being true that you couldn't have done anything else.

Defenders of OIC have different response strategies. First, they may just accept the Principle of Alternate Possibilities and reject Frankfurt cases. Next, they may deny the second premise. Maybe we are sometimes blameworthy for things that we are morally permitted to do if, for instance, it's an action that reflects a flawed moral character but is still morally permissible (for example, being curt with someone). Finally, they may deny the equivalence of the Principle of Alternate Possibilities and the conclusion of the argument as stated. Sometimes, the thought goes, you can not do one thing (for instance, you can refrain from doing it), but that doesn't mean there is something else that you can do. If you choose not to tell the cruel joke and the chip kicks in, you count as not telling the joke. That is, even though the chip will force you to tell the joke anyway, it won't be *you telling the joke* but the joke happening to you, as it were. So in this case, you can not tell the joke, but you can't yourself *perform some other action than telling the joke*. So if the chip doesn't kick in, it will be true that you are blameworthy for telling the cruel joke, but false that you could have done otherwise (i.e., performed some other action). Thus the Principle of Alternate Possibilities is false. But in that case, it will still be true that I can not tell the joke (because the joke will be happening to me; it won't be *my* action). So there is a way to deny the Principle of Alternate Possibilities while hanging onto the concluding line of the argument.

I won't take a firm stand on this argument here. But it's important to see that each of these responses has a long way to go before it is fully convincing. The first denies extremely plausible counterexamples. The second hangs on substantive and controversial normative ethical principles, and denies what many have taken to be a conceptual truth about blameworthiness. The last relies on a preferred view of action and agency, and so won't help those who don't share those views. Plus, it has itself come under serious criticism.

Some philosophers take the above argument to be a clear refutation of OIC. They argue that we should, on the strength of Frankfurt's examples, reject the Principle of Alternate Possibilities, and that rejecting it means rejecting OIC too. We've seen in this section that matters are a bit more complicated. Like the argument from moral dilemmas, this argument may be sound, but it is not the cleanest line to take against OIC because it depends on claims about which there is persistent and entrenched disagreement.[26]

We have now seen the major counterarguments and counterexamples to OIC. The list may seem scattershot, and space prevents me from mounting a full defense of any particular objection. Still, I hope to convey two points. First, if any of these objections succeeds at the end of the day, then OIC is sunk. Each one provides what would be, by itself, sufficient reason to reject it – if, that is, we really wanted to hold on to the phenomenon at the heart of the objection (e.g., the existence of moral dilemmas).

However, for many thinkers, one counterexample or counterargument to OIC is not enough. Because OIC has a lot to offer, there is a lot to lose by denying it. Better to reject whatever is causing the problem than to reject OIC. The second point takes this larger view seriously and turns it around. Looking at the motivations for denying OIC and objections to it, we can see that we lose a lot by adopting it, too. This allows the OIC denier to build a much stronger case against the principle. On the grand scale of reflective equilibrium, one or two of the above problems might weigh less heavily than OIC, which is, it must be admitted, itself an intuitively plausible principle. But taken together, they outweigh Standard OIC. Furthermore, though I haven't pursued it in detail here, many of the arguments can be recast as applying to OIC's major variants, and so present problems all around. So, while it hasn't been my aim to suggest that OIC is incoherent and therefore must be rejected, I have tried to show that it is not the self-evident principle that it is often claimed to be, and that accepting it is in fact quite costly.

3. Pragmatic Variations of OIC Rejected

Authors who reject OIC have frequently tried to find solace in one of two places: first, in blame-based principles, one of which we have just examined; and second, in pragmatic variations of OIC. Though I'll eventually argue that both are onto something important, I have more sympathy with the former camp than the latter. In this section, I'll explain why.

Recall from the previous chapter that the 'implies' of OIC is usually read as entailment. It is to this version that arguments in this chapter have been addressed. However, as we saw earlier, there are OIC-like principles that replace entailment with presupposition or conversational implicature. I will examine each one in turn, then close the section with a general remark about pragmatic OIC principles. (At this point, those readers who are relatively unfamiliar with these linguistic concepts are advised to revisit Chapter 1, Section 2.2.)

3.1 The Presupposition View

The presupposition view is very appealing. It shares with the entailment view that saying that someone ought to do something means that we think the person can do it. But it adds to this a further suggestion, i.e., that our saying that it's *false* that someone ought to do something also means we think the person can do it. It simply doesn't make sense to tell someone either that they ought to do something or that it's not true that they ought to do something unless we think they can do it. Why would we bother saying it at all?

Unfortunately, this view does not hold up to scrutiny. We can tell if one statement presupposes another with a few canonical tests. To keep things simple, I will focus on only one of these: *constancy under negation*. We can see this by looking again at cats and mats.

(1) My cat is on the mat.
(2) I have a cat.

If (1) actually does presuppose (2), then so should the negation of (1):

(~1) My cat is not on the mat.

This is constancy under negation. The important thing here is that, if (2) is false, then (~1) seems *just as strange to say* as (1). But this is not what we find in 'ought' statements. Let's look at Taylor.

(3) Taylor ought to help his mother.
(4) Taylor can help his mother.

It's a bit tricky to negate (3) because there's no nice way of negating English modal sentences in natural speech. "Taylor ought not help his mother," isn't the meaning we're after. We want something more along the lines of the following:

(~3a) It isn't the case that Taylor ought to help his mother.
(~3b) It isn't true that Taylor ought to help his mother.
(~3c) It's not like Taylor ought to help his mother.

It doesn't matter which we pick. None of these proposed negations presupposes (4). When we say that it *isn't* true that Taylor ought to help his mother, there is just no reason to think that he can help her. Simply put, the fact that one has no obligation to do something says absolutely nothing about whether one can do it.

This is connected to the use of OIC as a contrapositive principle. In most cases where we want to actually use OIC, we instead deploy its contrapositive, Cannot Implies Not-Ought. That is, we usually start from the fact that someone is unable to do something, and infer from this that they're under no obligation to do it. But to get contraposition, we need *both* the 'can' claim and the 'ought' claim to be false. In fact, we want the latter to follow in some way from the former. But this can't work on a presupposition view for the same reason that the negation test fails. If the negation test worked, we would find that, anytime we denied an 'ought' claim, we were presupposing the associated 'can' claim, and thus that they couldn't simultaneously be false. But in many cases precisely what we want is their simultaneous falsity. (The situation is especially bad for the semantic presupposition view. On this view, if the 'can' claim is false, then the 'ought' claim doesn't even get to have a truth-value, so contraposition certainly won't work.)

Though I think the presupposition view fails, at its core is an interesting thought to which we'll return in Chapter 4.

3.2 The Conversational Implicature View

Conversational implicature is even weaker than presupposition. When something is conversationally implicated, it's not part of the meaning of what we say, nor is it even entailed by what's said. Because it's not entailed, we can say the opposite of the thing implicated without speaking a contradiction. This phenomenon is called *cancelability*, a hallmark of conversational implicature. Using the earlier gas station example, if you tell me that you've run out of gas, and I reply, "There's a garage on the next street over, but unfortunately it's not open," I *cancel* the implicature. Notice that implicatures, but not entailments, are cancelable. If I say, "There's a garage on the next street over, but it's on this street," I say something that's obviously self-contradictory. That's because the garage's being on the next street *entails* that it's not on this street.

If the conversational implicature view is right, then 'can' is conversationally implicated by 'ought', but it's cancelable. For example, we often say things like, "I know I ought to, but I just can't," which feels a lot like a canceled conversational implicature. However, if 'ought' conversationally implicated 'can', how would we make sense of the central place of Cannot Implies Not-Ought? Conversational implicatures don't give us anything like contrapositives, and this is a serious problem. Take, for example, the following pairs, using '>' to indicate a conversational implicature.

"There's a garage around the corner," said in the context of the earlier conversation.
\> The garage is open and sells petrol.

"The garage isn't open and doesn't sell petrol," also said in that context.
⊁ There's not a garage around the corner.

Structurally, though, we would need this in order to capture OIC not only as a conditional but also as a contrapositive. In other words, we want both of the following implicatures:

"She ought to save the drowning child."
> She can save the drowning child.

"She cannot save the drowning child."
⊁ It's not true that she ought to save the drowning child.

But even if we grant that 'ought' conversationally implicates 'can', i.e., implicatures like the first of each pair here, we certainly don't get 'cannot' conversationally implicates 'not-ought', i.e., implicatures like the second. Drowning child cases aside, we use 'can' and 'cannot' language all the time. And many of the times we use 'cannot', nothing morally relevant is communicated at all. So, for example, if we are talking about our running times, and I say that I can't run a mile in under six minutes, nothing moral seems to be conversationally implicated. That I am not morally obligated to run a mile in under six minutes isn't an assumption that we make in order for the conversation to proceed cooperatively and efficiently. Most likely, none of the conversational participants have any thoughts about what I morally ought or ought not to do. So the conversational implicature view, like the presupposition view, ultimately fails to take seriously the fact that our paradigm appeals to OIC are *not* appeals to the conditional, but appeals to the contrapositive.

3.3 Pragmatic Views in General

Neither of these views looks promising. But it isn't just the particular concerns above that pose a problem. It's important to bear in mind that OIC crops up in places other than conversational contexts. It arises in deliberation as well. The point of any pragmatic account is to explain how we successfully communicate things that aren't explicitly said. A pragmatic account is thus fundamentally about interpersonal communication. But it would be a mistake to think that we use OIC exclusively interpersonally. We appeal to it in our thought as well. We can identify the very same patterns in how our beliefs about what we ought to do get excused or negated by inability.[27]

Even if we want to deny OIC, we cannot deny that OIC-like reasoning is ubiquitous. At the end of the day, the real challenge for the OIC denier is to provide an account that does justice to such phenomena, and to why people like OIC in the first place. The rest of the book will be devoted to articulating and responding to this challenge.

Notes

1. See Kant 1996.
2. There are two strategies for repairing this mismatch: to add degrees to the relevant 'ought', or to deny degrees to the relevant 'can'. For the former strategy, see Berg 2018.
3. See Stocker 1971, 311.
4. Matthew 5:48.
5. Romans 3:23.
6. This final way of framing the worry applies only to synchronic versions of OIC, and is therefore often used to motivate diachronic versions (see Chapter 1, Section 2.6). While it may be true that the stingy person cannot *now* give any money away, she could have done so.
7. Kramer 2016.
8. Hume 1978, 469 (3.1.1.27).
9. This is importantly distinct from the claim that one ought *not* to do something.
10. Some use this to argue against OIC as entailment and for a pragmatic account or a first-order moral account (Collingridge 1977, Statman 1995, Kühler 2012) or a metatheoretical account (Brown 1977). Bloomfield 2007 argues that a moral realist can avoid this conflict.
11. Buckwalter and Turri 2015, Chituc et al. 2016, and Mizrahi 2015.
12. Chituc et al. 2016, Henne et al. 2016.
13. Kurthy et al. 2017.
14. Austin 1956. See also Kramer 2005.
15. Darwall 2009, 26–27.
16. Hardimon 1994 explores this species of obligations.
17. For a fuller explanation, see Gowans 1987.
18. I've adapted this example from Tessman 2014.
19. For the view that moral dilemmas exist and falsify OIC, see Lemmon 1962, Sinnott-Armstrong 1988, DeLapp 2013, Tessman 2014, and Kramer 2016. For the view that there are no moral dilemmas because OIC is true, see Conee 1982, Herman 1996, and Zimmerman 1996.
20. This section summarizes the arguments presented in King 2014.
21. For a brief discussion of this, see Pereboom 1995, 36–37.
22. Many of the issues I discuss in this chapter deserve much more detailed treatment than I can offer here. This is especially true of the free will debate.
23. Although see Saka 2000 for the argument that the mere possibility of determinism is sufficient to undermine OIC as a conceptual principle.
24. Dahl 1974, Blum 2000.
25. Instead of blameworthiness, Frankfurt's version of the principle uses moral responsibility, which comprises both praise- and blameworthiness (1969).
26. Widerker first presented the argument from OIC to the Principle of Alternate Possibilities (1991). For more of the debate this spawned, see Copp 1997, Yaffe 1999, Saka 2000, Haji 2002, and Fischer 2003.
27. For a more thorough presentation of the arguments in this section, see King 2017.

3 Must Morality be Fair?

1. Motivating Thoughts

So far, I've argued that the standard version of OIC comes with a lot of very serious drawbacks. One natural line of response is that I've ignored some of its advantages, namely, the traditional motivations for the principle that often come up in the course of discussing it. There are three main motivations for adopting OIC. First is *fairness*, the idea that morality should be fair, and that OIC is one thing that keeps it that way. Second is *action-guidingness*, the idea that morality must guide action and that OIC ensures that it does so. Third and finally is what we could call *inference to the best explanation*. The idea here is that OIC is an essential part of the best explanation for certain patterns in moral thinking.

This chapter will look at fairness, and the next will look at action-guidingness and inference to the best explanation. These motivations have been advertised as presenting very serious reason to adopt OIC. We'll see that they don't provide as much support for OIC as it might seem. The first provides a little; the second provides none. But the third provides genuine and weighty reason to adopt OIC. Bearing all this in mind will give us a broader view of why we liked OIC in the first place, and what best fills its place once we deny it.

2. Fairness and Demandingness

2.1 Fairness

The fairness motivation starts from the compelling thought that morality should be fair. And it maintains that OIC is one thing (or *the* thing) that keeps it fair. It would be unfair to hold people responsible for wrongs that they couldn't have done anything to prevent. In situations where it looks like this might happen, we often say things like, "It wasn't her fault!" or

"He did all he could!" For there to be demands that we simply cannot satisfy seems somehow cruel. A just god, it seems, would not command the impossible of us, but would instead take our inabilities into account and calibrate commands accordingly.

In short, morality would be unfair if it demanded that we do things we cannot do. The most influential statement of this motivation comes from David Copp, who writes that "an adequate moral theory would imply or support the proposition that agent-requirements are morally unfair if the person required to act in a certain way is unable to act in that way."[1] Indeed, he thinks that a moral theory would be *incoherent* if it both said this and "failed to rule out" requirements to do the impossible. Therefore, he argues, any coherent moral theory must at least imply if not explicitly contain OIC.[2] "It is not intelligible to suppose that morality is itself morally unfair," he thinks.[3] So morality must be fair.

Others echo this sentiment. Robert Stern writes that it seems "unfair to attach such sanctions [for non-compliance] to an action that the agent cannot perform."[4] And Daniel Statman asks, "Why is it morally wrong to allow 'ought but cannot' statements? Because saying we ought to do x provides a powerful reason for blaming and even punishing us for not doing x. But this is unfair."[5] Fairness has also been used to motivate the impossibility of moral dilemmas. Michael Moore puts it this way: "it would be unfortunate for us in the extreme if morality often confronted us with [dilemmatic] choices."[6] The thought guiding all of these authors is that it would simply be unfair if morality demanded us to do things we cannot do.

2.2 Demandingness

There is a similar line of thought in debates about the demandingness of a moral theory (sometimes called overdemandingness), which concern how demanding a moral theory can be. Can a moral theory demand, for example, that we give up our daily cup of coffee and instead donate that money to charity? Maybe. But maybe only because this is a relatively weak demand. Can we also be required to give up an expensive education, phones, vehicles, hobbies, and homes and instead donate that money to charity? It's less clear. In these respects nearly all of us could survive on less. And we could use that money to provide mosquito nets, food, medicine, and safe drinking water to others who would not survive without them. But can morality demand so much of us?

Many think not. Bernard Williams writes, "It is absurd to demand" that people "should just step aside" from the projects that make their lives valuable.[7] The idea that a moral system could be disqualified for being too demanding is an influential objection to consequentialism.[8] And though the demandingness objection, as it has come to be known, is most often framed this way, it can also pose problems for non-consequentialist theories.

The resemblance between the demandingness objection and the fairness motivation for OIC is striking. It's clear that much of what lies behind the demandingness objection is something like fairness. A moral theory would be unfair if it demanded of us things that were very difficult or personally costly. Presenting these as arguments for their respective conclusions makes the parallel more vivid.

Fairness Argument for OIC:

P1. Moral theory M says that we ought when we can't (i.e., it violates OIC).
P2. If a moral theory says that we ought when we can't, then it is unfair.
P3. If a moral theory is unfair, then it is mistaken.
C. Therefore, M is mistaken.

This argument says that the correct moral theory must not violate OIC, because otherwise it would be unfair. This means, as Copp suggests, that the correct moral theory must in some sense imply or contain OIC. Next, to the demandingness objection.

Demandingness Objection (to consequentialism or any moral theory):

P1. Moral theory M demands too much of us.
P2. If a moral theory demands too much of us, then it is mistaken.
C. Therefore, M is mistaken.

This argument says that the correct moral theory must not be too demanding.

Setting aside for the moment whether these arguments are sound, we can see that premise 3 of the fairness argument mirrors premise 2 of the demandingness objection. The first states that if a moral view is *unfair*, then it is mistaken. The second states that if a moral view *demands too much* of us, then it is mistaken. But there is more that connects these two arguments.

Why is it that a moral theory that demands too much of us would be mistaken? What's wrong with a moral theory demanding an incredible degree of self-sacrifice? The thought may seem to be something like fairness. Thus one way to motivate premise 2 of the demandingness objection is to say that a moral theory that demands too much would be unfair, and thus mistaken. Interestingly, this means that demandingness objections provide an example of the fairness motivation cropping up outside OIC. Furthermore, the fairness argument above may also imply a cognate demandingness objection.

Why must a moral theory contain OIC? Because if it demanded us to do things that we couldn't do, it would demand too much.

It might be objected that I'm conflating different ideas. Worries about the demandingness of consequentialism are often put in terms of demands for *possible but unreasonable* sacrifices, e.g., of personal projects, relationships, or well-being. This is the "costs" reading of the demandingness objection: The costs of maximizing are too high. It might therefore seem like I'm drawing too tight a connection between demandingness and OIC.

Frequently, though, cases used to illustrate the demandingness objection blend costs together with difficulty, namely how difficult or easy it is to do the thing. To see the difference between costs and difficulty, compare the following cases. It is easy, but personally costly, for me to donate half of my income to charity. I know exactly how to do it – I just write a check or fill out an online form. Those actions are extremely easy to perform (they might even be extremely psychologically or motivationally easy for me, if I am very charitable). On the other hand, imagine a free throw contest for charity. It isn't personally costly to shoot free throws. All it costs is an afternoon. But it would be very difficult for someone who's bad at free throws.[9] It's demandingness in terms of difficulty that comes especially close to the fairness motivation for OIC.

Peter Vranas and Michael Kühler make similar points. Vranas says that there are two senses in which we might think that morality is too demanding. The first would be by "requiring us to do things that we find very *hard* to do, things that constitute significant *sacrifices*." Alternatively, it might be too demanding by "requiring us to do things that we literally *cannot* do, things that go beyond our *abilities*."[10] Similarly Kühler writes, "if an agent cannot do what he ought to do, it would *prima facie* be a matter of overdemandingness to uphold the 'ought' in question."[11]

I'm not suggesting that the fairness argument for OIC and the demandingness objection stand or fall together. A view would not be inconsistent, for instance, to uphold the fairness argument and deny the demandingness objection. It might hold that morality would be unfair to require us to do things we cannot do, but not unfair to require us to do things we can only do at significant personal cost. My point is that, on one way of understanding demandingness, there is a common underlying motivation for adopting OIC and adopting a not-too-demanding moral theory.

3. Against the Fairness Motivation

If I'm right, both arguments disqualify candidate moral theories for measuring unfavorably against the standard of fairness. But fairness is itself a normative, and plausibly even moral, standard. So one surprising feature of these arguments is that both hold moral theories as such to moral standards. This is very puzzling. It feels structurally problematic insofar as holding a moral theory to a particular *moral* standard looks circular. It presupposes a moral standard external or antecedent to the moral theory itself. I think this insight is basically right, and requires that we reconceive the role that the fairness motivation plays. But spelling all this out takes a bit of work.

3.1 Attempt 1: Agential Fairness

One thing we can be certain of is that people sometimes treat each other unfairly. Suppose that I give all students with glasses an A and fail all students without glasses, regardless of the quality of their work. In this situation, it is clear that I was unfair to the students.

Maybe we can think of morality's unfairness on this model. David Copp seems to have something like this in mind when he presents his fairness argument for OIC.

> It would be unfair to expect a person to do something, or to require that she do it, if she cannot do it. Similarly, morality would be unfair if it allowed that a person might be all-in morally required to do something that she cannot do – unless perhaps she cannot do it because of something she herself did at an earlier time that itself violated an all-in requirement. But it is not intelligible that morality might be unfair.[12]

Copp says that morality itself would be unfair if it demanded us to do things that we cannot do. But morality *must* be fair. Thus, morality must include OIC.

There is, however, a common response to the present way of reading Copp's argument.[13] Morality simply cannot be unfair in the way that I am unfair to my students. I am an agent, and because I am an agent, I am the sort of thing whose actions can be unfair. Morality is not an agent and does not act. To think of morality itself as being unfair is to make a category mistake.

More carefully, the passage above suggests that the fairness motivation is best rendered as *Agential Fairness*.

> *Agential Fairness*: Morality *qua* agent would be unfair if it demanded that we do things we cannot do.

In other words, morality would, in its capacity as an agent, treat us unfairly by demanding us to do things that we cannot do. This approach is obviously confused. Morality isn't an agent. Morality, the correct moral theory, is just a system of rules or guidelines. It doesn't sit down and say to you, "You must treat people equally!" To think of morality this way is to anthropomorphize it, to conceive of it as an agent. But it is not an agent and therefore cannot be fair or unfair in its dealings. Agential Fairness makes no sense. Notice also the cognate point to be made about the demandingness objection. If the demandingness objection is thought to suggest that morality *qua* agent would be unfair if it demanded us to do things that are too difficult or costly, then it faces the same problem.

Though it's of course true that morality is not an agent, this is not the silver bullet it is sometimes thought to be. Even if Copp's argument, as it stands, is best rendered as Agential Fairness, there are ways to avoid this superficial objection.

3.2 Attempt 2: Institutional Fairness

Morality is a system of rules, and systems of rules can be unfair too. Laws that give men more rights than women, for example, are paradigms of unfairness. Institutions that yield or incentivize corresponding preferential treatment are also unfair, even if they don't explicitly allow or promote such treatment.[14]

Suppose we think of morality on this model. Laws and institutions can be unfair, so maybe morality can be unfair in the same way. On this view, the fairness motivation is best rendered as Institutional Fairness:

> *Institutional Fairness*: The institution of morality would be unfair if it demanded us to do things we cannot.

So how exactly should we think of legal or institutional unfairness? For one, laws and institutions are created by humans. This might be thought to pose a problem to Institutional Fairness before it has even gotten off the ground. Maybe we haven't really escaped Agential Fairness. Consider a point made by Nomy Arpaly, who presents this worry as further support for her objection to Agential Fairness. She argues that we can only make sense of morality being fair or unfair if we think there is some celestial boss who dictates the moral rules. Then what we are really doing is accusing that boss (an agent) of being unfair.[15] By analogy, accusing an institution of being unfair only makes sense if what we're really doing is accusing the *creators* of that institution of being unfair. Thus, if morality doesn't have a creator, then Institutional Fairness doesn't make sense.

In calling a rule unfair, we often do mean to locate the unfairness ultimately in whoever created the rules. But that's not always the case. Sometimes we accuse rules, laws, and institutions of unfairness, even though we don't think that any particular person, or even any group of people, has been unfair. This sometimes happens when we see patterns emerge in systems of rules. These patterns may promote inequality, and in that case, we might well call the rules or structures that give rise to these patterns unfair. Inheritance laws might be seen this way. We might think the laws are unfair because they give rise to and reinforce inequality, but we need not thereby be accusing the people who wrote those laws of having been unfair. Maybe the laws weren't unfair then – maybe it took a very long time for the unfairness to emerge. Or maybe the laws aren't unfair under all circumstances – if everybody had equal amounts of wealth, equal access to resources, and equal financial vulnerability, then maybe inheritance laws would be fine. (The reality of this case is not so clean, but I hope that it illustrates what I mean.) In such cases, we might want to separate the unfairness of the rules themselves from any unfairness in their creators.

Can we understand morality, and therefore Institutional Fairness, on this more generous model? Unfortunately, I think this won't work either. There is a fundamental problem here. We assess the fairness or unfairness of laws or institutions by applying an independent moral standard to them. If they fail to meet that standard, we call them unfair. But we cannot apply an independent moral standard to morality itself.

This brings back the circularity worry in full force, so it's worth slowing things down a bit. To call something or someone unfair is to make a moral assessment. To say a moral rule is unfair is to say that it fails to meet certain *moral standards*, e.g., those related to equality. But how could that be? It *is* the moral standard.[16] Compare the famous example of the *mètre des Archives*, the platinum meter stick created to set the legal standard for the length of a meter in France. To say that this meter stick is too short or too long is to misunderstand its function. It is what other meter sticks are measured against; it is the very thing that sets the standard.

We can see the same problem in a different way. If a rule is unfair, this means at a minimum that it morally ought to be different. But then, if we accuse morality of unfairness for demanding of us things we cannot do, we are saying that morality morally ought to be different. But this is incoherent. It doesn't make sense to say that it's morally good that morality is the way it is, nor that it morally should be different. This is, to repeat, because morality sets the standard against which other things are morally measured. It cannot measure itself in this way. To say that the *mètre des Archives* is the exact length it *should* be seems to make a similar mistake.[17] It is simply the length that it is, and that is what defines a meter. Moral rules are what they are, and that is what defines what is morally right and wrong, good and bad, and fair and unfair.

This argument applies not only to fairness, but to any moralized motivation for preferring one moral theory over another. For instance, the motivation to adopt a particular moral system because justice, charity, or care requires that morality be a certain way is subject to the same structural worry. Furthermore, if we understand the demandingness objection as relying on fairness (and perhaps even if it doesn't), then it faces the same problem. A moral theory being assessed by independent moral standards makes no sense.

Modeling morality on laws or institutions therefore doesn't help us explain how to make sense of calling it unfair. Of course fairness applies to individuals, laws, and institutions. But it cannot apply to a *full moral system*. It simply doesn't make sense to call morality's dictates moral or immoral, and calling morality's dictates unfair does just this. Because fairness is itself a moral notion, it couldn't apply to a moral system, so to speak, from the outside.

3.3 Attempt 3: Fairness as a Substantive Moral Principle

The Fairness Argument we saw earlier essentially claims that, because morality would be unfair if it demanded us to do things we cannot, morality *does not* demand this. So far, we've been focusing on only one part of this argument (P2). We have seen that it doesn't make sense to accuse morality of unfairness, understood in either of the above two ways. But the other part of the argument (P3), which holds that a moral theory that is unfair would be mistaken – that it would somehow be disqualified as the right moral theory – is also clearly flawed. "It would be unfair if X, therefore not-X" is obviously bad reasoning, though surely the world would be a much nicer place if it were true.[18] To make sense of this inference that so many seem to make, we need to take a step back.

The attempts we have examined so far apply fairness as a first-order moral principle to morality itself. It's this structure that leads to many of the problems we saw above. The best way out of this is to try to construe fairness in some other way. Garrett Cullity seems to suggest something along these lines in the following passage:

> A standard I ought to meet is a standard I can properly be criticized for failing to meet. It is unfair to criticize me for not doing what I could not have done. So I cannot properly be criticized for not meeting a standard I could not have complied with, and such a standard is not one I ought to meet.[19]

There are two ways to interpret this suggestion. Read one way, OIC is a substantive moral claim; read another way, it is a pretheoretical constraint on moral theorizing. Each of these gives rise to different versions of the fairness motivation. We will look at the former in this section, and the latter in the next. We'll see that both interpretations are beset by problems. But because they best capture the spirit of the fairness motivation, these problems shed light on a number of issues at its core.

The former interpretation holds that morality demands something if and only if it is fair for one person to demand it of another. This is a substantive moral claim, one that would appear on a list of propositions that made up a moral theory. It says that the fact that it would be unfair for you to criticize me for a particular action means that the action is not morally required of me. Put another way, the fairness of interpersonal criticism provides conclusive evidence about our moral requirements.

On this reading, fairness is best rendered as Interpersonal Fairness.

> *Interpersonal Fairness*: It is fair for one person to demand that another person do something (or criticize another person for failing to do something) iff morality requires that person to do it.

For example, it's fair for you to demand that I donate more to charity if and only if morality requires me to donate to charity. Similarly, it's fair for you to criticize me for failing to donate more to charity if and only if morality requires me to do so.

We can use Interpersonal Fairness to support a version of OIC by combining it with the following claim.

> *Unfair Demands*: It is unfair for one person to demand that another person do what she cannot do (or to criticize another person for failing to do what she cannot do).

Together, these two claims entail that morality does not require that I do what I cannot do, that is, they entail OIC. Like Interpersonal Fairness, Unfair Demands is also a substantive moral principle – one about which actions are fair to demand. So the current argument makes OIC true, but as a substantive moral principle, one that stands or falls with other substantive moral principles. This makes the current version of OIC slightly different from Standard OIC, which is meant to be an analytic truth, one we can arrive at by thinking about the very concepts of 'ought' and 'can'.

It's also important not to conflate the version of OIC currently on the table with the Moral OIC principle introduced in Chapter 1 (Section 2.7). Moral OIC states that one morally ought not demand that another person do something if she cannot do it. The current version of OIC says, however, that morality does not require that we do what we cannot do. Notice, though, how similar Moral OIC is to Unfair Demands. If Unfair Demands is true, then Moral OIC is very likely also true.[20] And if the thought is that what makes it morally wrong to make unsatisfiable demands (i.e., what makes Moral OIC true) is that *it would be unfair*, then the two principles are effectively equivalent. But we can question both Interpersonal Fairness and Unfair Demands. Let's examine each in turn.

Interpersonal Fairness

First, Interpersonal Fairness overgenerates moral obligations. Suppose I'm teaching my friend how to drive a vehicle with a manual transmission. It is completely fair for me to criticize him for failing to shift at the right time. It is completely fair for me to demand that he release the clutch more slowly. But there's no moral requirement here. Morality doesn't demand that he release the clutch more slowly.

Even if we correct this by restricting Interpersonal Fairness to moralized demands, we run into a second problem. What makes a demand or criticism unfair has a lot to do with what the person making the demands is like, what other demands she makes, and what other circumstances are relevant. Some things are morally required, but are unfair to demand that someone do or to criticize someone for failing to do.[21] Let's assume that morality demands that we not lie. If I am a perpetual liar, is it fair for me to demand that you not lie? We often call hypocritical actions and attitudes like this unfair.[22] So it is, in at least one sense, unfair. Compare a similar case where someone criticizes women but not men for lying. In this case, does that person offer a fair criticism? In one sense, obviously not. It's unfair because women are held to a different standard than men.

Criticizing the victims of police entrapment also seems unfair. The then-criminal does something wrong, but only as a result of being led by police into a careful trap. Criticism seems unfair despite the fact that the criminal has done something wrong, even if the criminal act was fully voluntary and the criminal could have stepped away at any point with no repercussions. These cases complicate the equivalence of fair criticism and moral requirement.

Because demands and criticism can function as a form of punishment or public shaming, they can also be unfair if the moral transgression is relatively minor, understandable, or difficult to avoid. A demand itself is enough to create different attitudes in the target and those watching, to shift power balances, and to foster disdain and disapproval. But the mere fact that someone did something morally wrong may not warrant such a severe response.[23]

At its heart, the worry is that Interpersonal Fairness ignores interpersonal constraints on what's fair to demand or to criticize someone for doing. The reason there are such constraints is that demands and criticisms are ultimately interpersonal acts. To demand something of someone is not merely to take her to be morally required to do it, or even to be justified in that belief. To demand is to *do* something, and is therefore attended by contextual constraints. A customer may rightly believe that the cashier is morally required to give him correct change, but may choose not to demand correct change upon realizing that the cashier has slightly shorted him. The same is true of criticism. A boss may rightly believe that her employee is morally required not to embezzle money from the company's accounts, but may elect not to criticize the employee for embezzling. Perhaps she is waiting for violations to pile up so that she can press charges; perhaps she is afraid of confrontation; perhaps she is being blackmailed not to say anything. Such cases illustrate the social and highly contextual nature of demands and criticism.

Perhaps these cases are not fully convincing. A more charitable reading of Interpersonal Fairness takes demands and criticism not as *acts*, but as beliefs about obligations, and thus as abstracted away from these considerations. For those more inclined toward such charity, there is a different worry. It is possible to grant that Interpersonal Fairness is true, but deny that Interpersonal Fairness motivates OIC. Interpersonal Fairness offers a biconditional between the fairness of interpersonal demands and criticisms on the one hand and moral requirements on the other. However, Interpersonal Fairness will not motivate OIC if it's sometimes fair to demand (in the abstract sense) that others do things that they cannot. This brings us to the second contentious assumption of the argument: that it's always unfair to demand that someone do something they cannot.

Unfair Demands and Moral OIC

In order to assess Unfair Demands, we have to examine an aspect of the fairness motivation that we haven't yet touched on. In what sense of fairness are our demands and criticisms supposed to be fair or unfair? What exactly is the sense of fairness involved in the fairness motivation? In its clearest form, fairness has to do with egalitarianism. To be unfair is to treat people unequally for no good reason, whether by distributing goods unequally, offering unequal opportunities, or something else. For example, I don't act unfairly if I unequally distribute grades in a course, as long as those grades are unequally distributed for good reasons (because some students did the work, and did it well, while others didn't). But I act unfairly if I unequally distribute grades according to whether students wear glasses. This is the sense of fairness according to which it can seem unfair to criticize some but not all people. Here, what gets unequally distributed is moral praise and blame or moral demands. This is also, I suspect, at the heart of

Must Morality be Fair? 53

the hypocrisy charge: one asks more of others than of oneself, and therefore makes unequal demands.

But egalitarian fairness doesn't motivate OIC. Egalitarian fairness motivates principles according to which one ought not make different demands of different people in relevantly similar circumstances. But the fairness motivation for OIC must support the thought that it would be unfair to criticize someone, say, for not keeping a promise as a result of the inability to keep it, even if you criticized *anyone* who didn't keep a promise due to an inability. But if we're not talking about egalitarian fairness, then what are we talking about?

To demand that someone do something they cannot do seems to be unfair in that you don't, so to speak, give them a fighting chance. It's like a carnival game that has been rigged to be impossible to win, no matter how skilled you are. It is perfectly fair in the egalitarian sense: nobody can win. We are all equally bad in the eyes of the game. But it seems unfair in a further sense. The game is unfair because it is rigged. A law that demanded its citizens to cease breathing while they slept (even if it did so equally across its citizenry) would also be unfair in this way. It demands that they do something without concern for their situation, and in particular without concern for the fact that they cannot do the very thing it demands them to do. The law dooms them to failure. Maybe this is how we should understand the police entrapment model. Those entrapped didn't have the right kind of fighting chance. These people are not, we might say, "fair game" for criticism. Though it's hard to define exactly, I think this is much closer to the kind of fairness that is involved in the fairness motivation for OIC. Why is it unfair to demand that people do things that they cannot? Because that denies them a fighting chance to succeed. Instead, they're doomed to failure.

But the fairness motivation read this way doesn't seem to support OIC; it instead supports something like the Principle of Alternate Possibilities[24] or, more likely, a principle connecting moral responsibility and blameworthiness to ill will. Frankfurt cases are illuminating on this score. If you intentionally make a cruel joke, you're blameworthy for doing so, even if the chip in your brain would have kicked in and forced you to make the joke regardless. Here, it also seems fair to criticize you for making a cruel joke. And it seems fair despite the fact that you didn't have a fighting chance not to make it, because you're the one who is responsible for making it. The fact is that the chip didn't kick in, and you are properly criticizable for what you did. The joker *intentionally* does something cruel. In cases like this, the fairness of criticism tracks ill will and intentionality rather than the ability to do otherwise. A principle like this also has the resources to explain why it seems perfectly fair to criticize those who are culpably unable to do what they ought. The self-sabotager *intentionally* acts so as to make herself unable to fulfill the obligation.[25]

A final attempt might be made to rescue Unfair Demands. Maybe *criticism* is fair in situations like these. Still, it's unfair to *demand* that the jokemaker not tell the cruel joke or that the self-sabotager pay back the debt. Or, as Moral OIC has it, it's morally impermissible to demand that people do things they cannot do. Recall that we're currently understanding demands in an abstract sense, where demanding something of someone is simply holding that there's a moral requirement that applies to that person. In other words, I demand something of you just in case I think you are morally required to do it. Now we must ask whether it's always unfair or morally impermissible to demand that others do what they cannot.

There are two ways to respond. First, we may agree that it's not fair to make such demands, but deny that this is relevant to determining the presence of a moral obligation. This concedes Unfair Demands, but denies Interpersonal Fairness, thus blocking the argument from fairness to OIC. (This line is taken by those who defend Moral OIC while denying OIC.) Alternatively, we may claim that it is perfectly fair to demand that people do what they cannot. Such a person can be fair game for demands. After all, what could be unfair or morally inappropriate about regarding there to be an obligation when that obligation in fact exists? If a friend promises to pick up your dry cleaning, there's nothing unfair about simply regarding there to be an obligation present, and in that sense holding them to that demand, bearing in mind that this doesn't say anything about how you should actually act in whatever situations arise.

In the end, Interpersonal Fairness trades on an ambiguity. Demands and criticism, understood as interpersonal acts, are sometimes unfair when people are unable to comply. But the best explanation of that unfairness is not inability, since many things make interpersonal acts unfair, and it's sometimes perfectly fair to condemn actions someone could not avoid. Alternatively, demands and criticism in the abstract sense either support a principle about blameworthiness rather than OIC, or else depend on Unfair Demands – a claim there's good reason to believe to be false.

3.4 Attempt 4: Fairness as a Pretheoretical Constraint

Earlier, we briefly saw that there were two ways to interpret Cullity's remarks. The former interpretation led us to Interpersonal Fairness, which faces problems on several fronts. On the latter interpretation, however, fairness acts as a pretheoretical constraint on the development of a moral theory. Fairness is an intuitive data point that a moral theory cannot violate. It's a constraint that governs moral theory building, or evidence of what the correct moral theory would say. Compare our treatment of certain moral fixed points: A moral theory simply cannot demand that we harm innocents for the sheer fun of it. A moral theory simply cannot base human rights on skin color. Similarly, a moral theory simply cannot be unfair.

To understand this view better, let's step away from morality for a moment and think about theorizing in general. Roughly speaking, our best, most accurate theories are either things that we have discovered about the world, i.e., things that truly describe how the world works; or things that we have created, i.e., mere inventions of ours. Either type of theory will be subject to pretheoretical constraints. For example, if a theory of physics is aimed at describing how the world really works, then the data will provide an important piece of evidence that a given theory is the true one. If on the other hand a theory is not aimed at discovering truths, but instead is wholly created by us, then pretheoretical constraints are regulatory principles constraining what we want our theory to look like. If we are constructing a theory of physics, then we want it to be useful, and a useful theory must be consistent with the data. Either way, data forms a pretheoretical constraint on physics.

On the present interpretation, we should think of fairness as playing a role in moral theorizing that is analogous to the role data plays in scientific theorizing. Fairness is a kind of data point in moral theory building that either is evidence for what the correct moral theory looks like or regulates what we want our moral theory to look like.

This is the interpretation that I think best captures what the fairness motivation really is.

Pretheoretical Fairness: A moral theory must be designed so that it is fair.

In this form, fairness admittedly has a question-begging flavor, but no more so than any other pretheoretical constraint on a theory. Is it question begging to say that no moral theory can demand that we harm innocents for fun? If it is, it's not harmfully so. The structure of this position is that some things function as data for a moral theory to be built around. And this structure, unlike the structures of Agential and Institutional Fairness, isn't itself problematic.

But there are two further stances that the OIC defender needs to take for Pretheoretical Fairness to motivate OIC. One is that fairness can – and does – constrain moral theorizing, and the other is that OIC is required for fairness in the relevant sense. It may be, for example, that we want the theory to be fair in the egalitarian sense, but OIC isn't required for fairness in that sense. Rather, it is fairness in the fighting chance or fair game sense that's connected to OIC.

The OIC denier might reject either of these claims. Rejecting the latter, that OIC is required for fairness in this sense, doesn't strike me as a promising path. Rejecting the former, that fairness can constrain a moral theory, is better. After all, there's no agent who created it, and we don't have some other independent moral theory by which to assess it. But there might be reasonable responses here. It seems like the OIC denier is a bit too unyielding if she rejects these claims. We learn more if we grant that a moral theory can be unfair in this sense, and that Pretheoretical Fairness doesn't fall prey to these worries, because we must still ask whether and to what extent fairness does constrain our moral theory.

There seems to be something to the thought that morality should give us a fighting chance. Morality shouldn't feel like a rigged game. But this is a pretheoretical motivation, and so does not suffice for adopting OIC, any more than any data suffice for adopting a theory that explains them. It only weighs in OIC's favor. Several considerations weaken its strength. First, once we separate the unfairness of certain interpersonal demands and criticism, the force of Pretheoretical Fairness is weakened. Next, morality clearly makes demands of our mental states and character, and such states are sometimes indisputably unavoidable. This undermines any reason we had to think that we must have a fighting chance to meet all of morality's demands. Furthermore, there are various ways for moral theories to soften the unfairness blow. If a moral theory allows that we can do better or worse, even in failing to do something we ought, then it looks much less unfair to make unsatisfiable demands. Finally, examples like those from Chapter 2 give us reason to think that a moral theory actually need not give us a fighting chance to fulfill our obligations. Someone who is caught in a moral dilemma, for example, just doesn't need to have a fighting chance to do both things in order to be morally required to do them. Nor does someone who makes an unsatisfiable promise or signs a contract that becomes unfulfillable.

At the end of the day, though, what's left of Pretheoretical Fairness weighs genuinely in favor of OIC. But it motivates other, related principles as well. It motivates various epistemically bounded principles. Peter Graham has labeled one such principle OIE: Ought Implies Evidence.[26] OIE states that, if someone ought to do something, then they have evidence that they ought to do it. Though it parallels OIC in some ways, OIE isn't quite a variant of OIC, since nothing like 'can' appears in the consequent. Why does Pretheoretical Fairness motivate this? Because, if people don't have any evidence that they ought to do something, then they don't have a fighting chance to get it right. They can only luck into fulfilling their obligations. Similarly, a subjective ought sits more naturally alongside fairness than an objective one. What matters are one's (perhaps reasonable) beliefs, not the actual state of affairs.

In fact, if we take a permissive view of what it means to give people a fighting chance, we should take other features of their psychologies into account, as well as their other values and priorities. If we really want to give people a fighting chance to get things morally right with any consistency, we might need to lower our moral bar. Here we return to the demandingness objection. Does a strong version of act utilitarianism give people a fighting chance to fulfill all of their obligations? Viewed one way, it does; but viewed another, it doesn't because it's simply too demanding. Regardless of whether they *can* give up so much (in the sense that's relevant to OIC), people are not the sorts of creatures that *will* do so. In order to give people a fighting chance to fulfill their moral obligations, then, we need to lower the moral bar, so that moral obligations are more realistic and achievable. This very strategy is occasionally taken by rule consequentialists. Morality cannot be very demanding because, if it were truly that demanding, people wouldn't internalize or comply with the rules as fully. They would, in response to very demanding rules, do worse than they would were the rules a bit easier to satisfy.[27]

Here we see again how fairness and demandingness concerns bleed together. And even though Pretheoretical Fairness motivates all of these principles, it does so only rather weakly, and there may well be other reasons to reject them (as is plausibly the case with OIE). I think we should still reject OIC, but it's important to keep in full view what we lose when we lose it, so that we might better accommodate that loss. A complete moral theory should try to recapture as much fairness as possible, and in the next chapter, I'll suggest some ways to do so.

Notes

1 Copp 2003, 272 (see also Copp 2008, 71).
2 Copp 2003, 272.
3 Copp 2003, 274.
4 Stern 2016, 102.
5 Statman 1995, 44.
6 Moore 2007, 37–38.
7 Williams 1973, 116. Brandt also argues that an overly demanding moral theory "can hardly be taken seriously: like the Sermon on the Mount, it is a morality only for saints" (1998, 276). Benn calls this the "Extreme Demands Objection" (2016, 69).
8 Consequentialist theories hold that one ought to perform the action that will produce the best overall consequences. These theories often require us to give up many, if not all, of the things mentioned in the previous paragraph.
9 See McElwee 2016 for more on this distinction, and Nelkin 2016 for a discussion of difficulty.
10 Vranas 2007, 196–197.

11 Kühler 2016, 127.
12 Copp 2008, 71.
13 See Arpaly 2006, 107, van Someren Greve 2014.
14 This does not imply that things like affirmative action laws are unfair, since such laws are meant to correct for past or ongoing unfairness.
15 Arpaly 2006, 107.
16 See also van Someren Greve 2014.
17 Unless we assume a *different and independent* standard of metric length, as they did in selecting the particular platinum bar that became the *mètre des Archives*.
18 See also van Someren Greve 2014, who argues that such a schema proves too much.
19 Cullity 2016, 147–148.
20 The only hitch is that making such a demand of someone could be unfair, but still be a true claim about what they ought to do. I suspect that those who defend Moral OIC will be uncomfortable allowing such cases.
21 Some, following J.S. Mill, may want to tie moral wrongness very tightly to demands:

> We do not call anything wrong, unless we mean to imply that a person ought to be punished in some way or other for doing it; if not by law, by the opinion of his fellow-creatures; if not by opinion, by the reproaches of his own conscience.
>
> (1987, 321 (V.14))

What follows in this section can be seen as an extended counterargument to the view Mill presents here.

22 For a similar point about fairness and hypocrisy, see van Someren Greve 2014.
23 This may recall our earlier discussion of excuses (Chapter 2, Section 2.3), which occur when a wrongdoer has an excuse and therefore isn't blameworthy. These cases, however, are meant to grant some degree of blameworthiness and call into question the justifiability of our associated interpersonal demands and criticism.
24 As a reminder, this is the principle that, if someone is blameworthy for something, then one can not do it. See Chapter 2, Section 2.8.
25 In cases where the disabling action is done as a result of neglect rather than ill will, nevertheless the person lacks sufficient forethought, and this is what enables fair criticism.
26 Graham 2011, 365ff.
27 For example, Arthur uses this to argue that the "ideal moral code" wouldn't demand that people give up all their wages to global famine relief (2007, 629).

4 Toward a Better Explanation

1. Action-Guidingness and Pointlessness

It is the very nature of a moral system to be practical. But if morality tells us to do something that we cannot do, it apparently fails in this regard. It only tells us that we will inevitably fail to do what we morally ought to do. But just knowing that cannot help me in my actual practical deliberations about my next course of action. On the other hand, if OIC is true, then morality is constrained to demand of me only things that I can do. In that case, OIC would help me decide what to do. It would inform my deliberations by pointing to the concrete thing that I both ought to do and can do. OIC therefore helps to ensure the action-guidingness and essential practicality of morality. This is how action-guidingness is meant to support OIC.

The canonical statement of this also appears in Copp's work:

> Moral requirements are action-guiding. That is, their point is to guide agents' decisions among their alternatives. All-in requirements partition an agent's alternatives at the point of action into those that are permissible and those that are not. Hence, knowledge of what one is all-in morally required to do enables one to select a permissible action from among one's alternatives. Given this, an adequate theory would imply that an agent is all-in morally required to do A only if she can do A. Otherwise, a permissible action would not be among her alternatives, since a person's alternatives at a time are the things she can do at that time.[1]

The argument is that morality must be able to guide decisions about what to do. And morality could not do this unless there were some permissible action among our alternatives. But denying OIC means saying that there's sometimes no permissible action among our alternatives. What we really ought to do, we cannot do. So, in order for morality to guide our decisions about what to do, OIC must be true.

Copp calls this "an argument from the point of moral requirements."[2] As such, this motivation is sometimes cast in terms of *pointlessness*. Many have thought that morality would be pointless if it demanded us to do things that we could not do.[3] By retaining OIC, we ensure that morality never makes pointless demands. So what we see are two slightly different motivations: action-guidingness and pointlessness.

These aren't quite the same, though. To illustrate the difference, imagine a god who commands us to do things we cannot do. This seems ridiculous. Why? Because that command cannot direct our action. It's pointless. "But what do I do now?" you might wonder. "Why bother telling me to do that if you know I can't?" Compare also a god who commands us to do things that we cannot *but* do. For example, this god commands us to refrain from tripping people on faraway sidewalks. This also strikes many as ridiculous. It's pointless to demand things that we cannot help but do. In a sense, this won't help guide our action, either. But this god passes Copp's action-guidingness test. In his (and thus our) sense, morality can be action-guiding if it tells us that we must do something even when we cannot but do it, since it still gives us a permissible action among our alternatives. Pointlessness, however, appears to apply to both sets of commands: those requiring us to do things we cannot do, as well as those requiring us to do things we cannot but do. It thus can be seen to motivate both OIC and OICA.

So, although action-guidingness and pointlessness are very similar, they are sometimes used to motivate OIC in slightly different forms. Action-guidingness motivates Standard OIC by holding that morality must guide action. Pointlessness is sometimes used this way, but more paradigmatically says that moral *demands* or *statements* (and perhaps judgments) must have a point. Proponents of the pointlessness motivation often direct themselves toward how unusual or strange it would be to *say* that someone should do something that they couldn't do, rather than how unusual or strange it would be for *morality* to require that someone do something that they couldn't do. Pointlessness is therefore more frequently used to motivate pragmatic variants of OIC.[4]

Presented this way, the pointlessness motivation is perfectly compatible with denying Standard OIC. Pointlessness could also motivate OIC itself, though, if we thought that the strangeness of moral demands that violate OIC were evidence of OIC's truth.[5] Sometimes accompanying the pointlessness charge is the claim that unfulfillable demands are not just pointless, but immoral. Here the fairness motivation starts to creep back in. To keep these distinct, bear in mind that pointlessness is ultimately about the inappropriateness or even the irrationality of making an unsatisfiable demand. To suggest that this inappropriateness or irrationality would *also* be immoral requires a further argumentative step. Some authors have made this further step, defending a pragmatic version of OIC together with Moral OIC.[6]

Our current concern is not, however, whether any of these OIC principles are true. Our current concern is with how OIC is motivated. The pointlessness motivation usually focuses on the pointlessness of moral claims or statements. It has been used to motivate OIC in both its standard and pragmatic forms. Action-guidingness, on the other hand, typically motivates OIC as traditionally interpreted: a true principle that tethers our moral obligations to our abilities. The next two sections will respond to these motivations directly by showing which aspects of these motivations we should (and shouldn't) take seriously.

2. Against Pointlessness

Let's look first at pointlessness when used to motivate Standard OIC. The problem with the pointlessness motivation used this way is that, even if a statement is pointless, it need not be false.[7] If a friend and I are deciding whether to have sandwiches or sushi for lunch, and I tell her that my mother makes delicious dumplings, I say something completely pointless. My mother isn't nearby; having her dumplings is not an option that's on the table. That doesn't make it *false* that she makes delicious dumplings. In fact, I assure you that it's true. All sorts of statements are like this. Similarly, maybe you ought to do something you cannot, but saying so would be pointless. We can even allow that the reason it's pointless to say is because you can't do it. But that doesn't mean that it's false that you ought to. So pointlessness doesn't support Standard OIC. It only supports the view that it's pointless to *say* that someone do something when she cannot, i.e., OIC as a pragmatic principle.

The rest of the worries cut more deeply against the pointlessness motivation, regardless of which incarnation of OIC it is used to motivate. They each highlight different ways in which there *is* a point to saying that someone ought to do something, even if they cannot. Paul Saka, for instance, writes that "there can be good reason to demand the impossible from you, as when such demands will spur you on to superior performance."[8] How many parents have told their children to do things, fully aware that they can't, in order to watch them develop, learn, and improve? Adults are not so different from children. When told we must do something, even if it's true that we cannot, we sometimes come much closer to doing it than we otherwise would.

A separate class of cases illustrates another point that such statements can have: they can increase our moral humility. Taking one Christian perspective, Robert Stern argues that God's demands that we do things we cannot do demonstrates God's "forgiveness and the power of grace, or . . . show[s] us something about our limitations as human beings."[9] In other words, when Jesus says, "Be ye therefore perfect," and correspondingly when we reiterate that to each other, the purpose of this is to remind us that, despite our inability to do something, we receive divine forgiveness and mercy. It puts us in our place as fallible and limited human beings.

One doesn't need to buy into a religious worldview to recognize the force of this thought. It can be secularized. Christopher Jay argues that, in cases where someone cannot do what she ought, "the *point* of telling her what she ought to do [is] to show her . . . that *because she cannot do as she ought to* she must stop thinking of herself as . . . a paragon of virtue."[10] There isn't a deity demanding that we do things, but being told that we ought to do things, even when we cannot, puts us in our place as fallible and limited human beings. By increasing our moral humility, these Christian and secular cases illustrate another way that telling people that they ought to do things when they cannot can have a point.

There are also much less dramatic ways in which such statements can have a point. If a friend of yours has forgotten that he was supposed to be at a meeting this afternoon, you might remind him that he ought to be there, even if you both know that he can't get there in time. Saying this is far from pointless. He may decide that he ought to call or rush to get there, even if he'll be late. He may decide that there's nothing to be done about this meeting, but that he had better get a more reliable system of tracking his appointments so this doesn't happen in the future. Maybe the point is to get a quick jab in, if he had just been bragging about how he never misses meetings. Maybe the point is to celebrate, if he had intended all along to snub others by skipping it. All we need to do to turn pointless statements into appropriate ones is to get creative.[11]

So we shouldn't take the pointlessness motivation seriously. Telling people that they ought to do things that they cannot serves many purposes, both lofty and mundane. Of course there are times when saying so will be pointless, but the pointlessness motivation gets its force by claiming that this is always the case, which is simply not true. However, the fact that such statements can be useful isn't evidence that OIC is false, either. That it's sometimes good to be told or believe false things is an insight that we all come to at some point in our lives. So even someone interested in defending OIC can accept many of these cases and yet remind us that saying false things (as that someone ought to do something even if they cannot) can have a point. The point is to get people to do the best that they *can* do, which is all that they *ought* to do, such a defense would go. The upshot is that pointlessness doesn't motivate OIC in its standard form, but it doesn't motivate a denial of OIC either. It is simply irrelevant.

Compare what we might say about speech acts like advising. It is typically inappropriate to advise someone to do something that she cannot do.

And it's usually, if not always, disingenuous to advise someone to do something that you *believe* she cannot do, even if in fact she can. This might seem to support OIC. Perhaps it best explains why advice like this is inappropriate. But this is unlikely. Advising is an interpersonal act, and as such, many things affect its appropriateness. It can be appropriate to advise someone to do something they cannot do, if such advice will get them closer to doing what's right. But it can also be appropriate to advise someone to do something that's immoral, if that advice will prevent them from doing something even worse, or if it's known that the advisee is likely to do the opposite of what's recommended. Very different things make advice good or appropriate than make moral propositions true.

Pointlessness may motivate a limited pragmatic version of OIC. Not all pragmatic views will be licensed. A semantic presupposition view, for example, will have a lot of difficulty accommodating the above phenomena. But perhaps a limited pragmatic version, in which one's inability factors into what it's appropriate to say, is supported by pointlessness. Such a version wouldn't present an exceptionless rule, but would highlight one's inability to do something as a factor in what it's appropriate to say. But what one is and isn't able to do is often relevant in pragmatics, so this particular incarnation of OIC, if we even want to call it that anymore, should come as no surprise at all.

3. Against Action-Guidingness

Action-guidingness is a close cousin of pointlessness. The thought is that morality must guide action, and OIC is necessary for morality to guide action. Thus, OIC must be true.

There's an important question about what action-guidingness means, and we can start to see this by looking at the cases of moral humility discussed above. Why think that a moral theory fails to do all it should if it tells you that what you've done or what you're doing is unavoidably wrong? A moral theory that always does this – that is, tells you that *everything* you do is unavoidably wrong and that you can never do any better than you in fact do – does not seem to guide action. What, though, if it tells you what to do most of the time, but tells you that you unavoidably do wrong in certain situations?[12]

The issue here is one about the meaning of action-guidingness. Is a moral theory action-guiding if it *does* guide action? In other words, is a moral theory action-guiding if it guides *some* actions? Or is a moral theory action-guiding only when it guides *all* actions?[13] The former is fully compatible with denying OIC, even if we assume that whenever it violates OIC, morality fails to guide action. Even if morality sometimes fails to guide action, it can still be true that it does generally guide action. Morality can still be action-guiding in a very important sense.

If morality must guide all actions in order to count as action-guiding, then action-guidingness faces problems from another quarter of moral thought. If there is something morally required of you, say, donating 5% of your income to charity, but also something supererogatory you could do, namely donating 5.5% or 6% or . . . then what exactly does morality say that you should do? If morality as action-guiding must present us with one unique action in every morally loaded situation, what is the unique action you ought to perform in this situation? There isn't one. There are different ways of satisfying your obligation, some of which are morally better than others. Morality permits you to do any of these, even if it tells you that some are better.

But perhaps morality doesn't need to give us one unique action to perform in order to count as action-guiding. Maybe all it needs to do is provide at least one permissible action. This seems to be Copp's suggestion. But there are good reasons to think that this is too narrow to be a plausible conception of action-guidingness.[14] Morality can guide action even when there's no permissible action at all.

Many of the cases from the previous section can be adapted to illustrate this. It's not as if Christians are utterly baffled when Jesus commands perfection, while other Biblical passages deny the possibility of human perfection. It may even be that the aim of perfection provides more action guidance than other aims, since there are always improvements to be made. The secular version has parallel action-guiding upshots, apparent in the case of the man above who's currently missing his meeting. Once he knows that he is currently failing to fulfill an obligation, he may come to recognize other things he should be doing, whether that's apologizing, rushing to get there late, or planning better for the future. Here is a case where morality guides action, despite a violation of OIC. Your friend ought to do something he cannot, and yet morality still gives him some instruction.

We can formulate a class of examples where you ought to do one thing, but as a result of failing to do that (whether by choice or because you can't), you ought to do something else. Following Ulrike Heuer, we'll call the former non-derivative oughts and the latter derivative oughts.[15] Let's assume that we non-derivatively ought to keep our promises. If we fail to keep them, whether willfully or not, we incur derivative obligations. We ought to apologize for our failures or even offer compensation for the broken promise, when that's appropriate. Similarly, it sometimes seems like we ought to do things that we cannot yet do. A judge ought to make unbiased decisions; a teacher ought to explain the subject matter clearly; and each of us ought to act kindly to one another. But an exhausted judge may fall into bad patterns;

a teacher covering something new may be unable to explain it clearly; and there are times when each of us will be too distracted, apathetic, or ill-tempered to act kindly. These are analyzable in the same way. Because, for example, each of us non-derivatively ought to act kindly, we derivatively ought to practice and actively develop our patience, sympathy, and compassion toward others so that we might enable kinder actions in the future.

These examples show that the conception of action-guidingness as presenting us with at least one permissible action to perform is too narrow. Morality can guide action even if there's no permissible action to perform. Morality very plausibly has the layered demands we've been discussing, so there's no reason to think that, if we had no permissible actions available, we'd get absolutely no guidance from morality.

To say that a denial of OIC undermines action-guidingness involves an overly simplistic conception of what a moral system looks like. It ignores the richness of moral thought. In fact, explaining the full experience of such demands is harder if one holds on to OIC. By maintaining OIC, one denies that the teacher who cannot explain the subject matter is under any obligation to do so, or that the person who is too cranky to act kindly ought to do so. If such people aren't failing to do something that they ought to be doing, then how do we explain the strong feeling that they ought to take steps to improve? One common reply is that it would be better if the teacher could explain things better and it would be better if the curmudgeon could act kindly. But that doesn't seem to capture the claim morality seems to have on these people. It's not merely that it would be better this way, in the sense that it would be better if there were world peace. It's something stronger. These people are responsible for causing harm; and it is their responsibility to improve.[16]

This section has not denied that morality must be action-guiding, or even that morality is essentially action-guiding. But it has denied that morality's action-guidingness motivates OIC. There are many ways and many situations in which morality can guide action without conforming to OIC.

Furthermore, like fairness, action-guidingness motivates what I referred to in the previous chapter as epistemically bounded principles, i.e., those that take into account things like beliefs, justification, or access to evidence. According to Copp, morality has to help us decide what to do. I've argued that it helps us decide what to do even if it doesn't give us at least one (or one unique) permissible action to perform. But it cannot help us decide what to do if we don't have any evidence of what morality says, or if we don't know what to do to pursue moral ideals. To see what I mean, compare two possible scenarios.

For the first, suppose that we have a set of moral rules, and that OIC is true. Not only this, but suppose also that the moral rules make it so that, in every situation, there is one and only one permissible action. It is, therefore, morally required. Unfortunately, in this scenario we have no access to the moral rules. They're true, but we have no way of knowing what they are, or even if we did, how we would go about satisfying them. (Think of a version of maximizing act utilitarianism where the only moral rule is to do what maximizes utility, combined with the assumption that we don't actually have any way to figure out what would maximize it.) For the second, suppose that we have a set of moral rules, but that OIC is false. There are some situations in which no action is morally permissible; we're doomed to moral failure. Nevertheless some options are still morally better than others. We may even know how we would go about training ourselves to better enable obligation fulfillment in the future. Finally, in this scenario we have access to the moral rules.

Of these two theories, it's the second, not the first, that is action-guiding. The first can't guide action at all. It doesn't help us decide what to do because we're not epistemically positioned to reliably do what we ought. At best we'll luck into it. The second, however, gives us lots of moral advice and guidance, despite telling us that we will sometimes (if not frequently) fail to do all we ought. We still have epistemic access to what it is that we ought to do, and how to do it. Even if we can't do the right thing now, we know how to go about improving ourselves in order to do what we ought. So action-guidingness, like fairness, better supports some kind of epistemically bounded principle concerning our 'oughts' or blameworthiness. It does not support Standard OIC.

4. Inference to the Best Explanation

The third and final motivation for OIC is an inference to the best explanation. Inference to the best explanation arguments take a set of data that could, in principle, be explained by several different theories, and hold that we should adopt the theory that offers the best explanation. Two examples will help clarify how this sort of point has been deployed in support of OIC.

The first is that it's simply not true that I ought to snap my fingers and thereby make all the suffering in the world disappear.[17] Second, if we suppose a child is drowning fifty miles away from where you currently are, it isn't true that you ought to save him. In these cases, not only does it seem like you've done nothing wrong (by not so snapping or saving), but our sense is that it seems that way *because* you can't perform the relevant actions. So not only does OIC provide the right answers, but it appears to provide the right reasons for those answers. The finger snapping example seems right precisely because I can't make world suffering disappear by snapping my fingers. If I could do it, it seems like I *would* be obligated to. This suggests that OIC is at work. It is the same with the second case. Here, too, it is false that you ought to save the child, and that seems to be true because there's no way for you to get there in time to save him. But if you were right at the shore watching this happen (barring other complications), you would have that obligation. In other words, it's not just that in these cases (1) you can't do something and (2) it's false that you ought to do it. But (1) and (2) seem to be importantly related facts. Why? Because *if* you could do it, *then* it would be true that you ought to. The 'cannot' is precisely what precludes the 'ought' from arising.

An influential subclass of examples further stress this point. We might call these the *No Absurd Oughts*[18] cases. Nobody has the moral obligation to travel back in time and stop the Holocaust. (In fact, nobody has the moral obligation to travel back in time and do anything.) Why? The most natural explanation, and indeed the one that seems completely obvious, is because no one can do that.

The problem is that, if OIC isn't true, then we cannot block those obligations from arising. We would have all kinds of obligations. Maybe you ought to run faster than the speed of sound to save someone's life; maybe a doctor in the eighteenth century ought to administer penicillin; maybe someone with paralyzed limbs ought to swim out and save someone who is drowning; maybe I ought to travel back in time and stop the Holocaust. To think that we ought to do these things, though, is absurd. So we need some way to block these obligations, and OIC seems to fit the bill perfectly. And if OIC does not block these, then what else can?[19]

5. Against the Best Explanation Motivation

This is the most powerful motivation for OIC, though it's the least frequently discussed of the three motivations we've looked at. However, given its structure, we might instead call it *supporting intuitions*. Once we notice that these are equivalent, we can see that this is a very common motivation to rely on, albeit not always explicitly.

An initial accusation is that this motivation is question begging. After all, if the OIC denier doesn't share the OIC-favoring intuitions, then repeating those intuitions and underscoring that they do indeed favor OIC does not produce a position that's dialectically effective. It's not going to convince anyone who's not already convinced. I think such a knee-jerk reaction is uncharitable. OIC-favoring intuitions, embodied in the cases above, really are quite strong. It's easy to forget this when we're focusing on trickier aspects of the debate like moral dilemmas, subtle time indexing, or the pragmatics of speech, but here, I think, we really do give something up when we give up OIC. We give up a simple, powerful, and incredibly intuitive explanation.

A stronger worry takes more circumspect form. Any inference to the best explanation argument takes a set of data and says of that set that the best explanation is X, and that we should therefore believe X or have our theory include X. And although the best explanation of the above cases is OIC, those cases provide only a limited set of data. It ignores, for example, all the cases we talked about in Chapter 2.

Best explanation arguments are, in technical terms, non-monotonic. Their conclusions, in other words, are not decisive. It's possible to add evidence or premises so that some of the conclusions that were previously licensed would no longer be licensed. This is how virtually all scientific theorizing works. I have a set of data that the supposition X best explains, and therefore posit that X. But adding further data could make Y, rather than X, the best explanation. So, for example, before Galileo, we had a set of data that was best (most simply and powerfully) explained by geocentrism. After Galileo, we had more data, and a better theory that could explain all of the data: heliocentrism. It made certain calculations more complicated. It also meant that some of our naked-eye observations were misleading. But it was a much better explanation on the whole.

While OIC really is an excellent explanation of the above cases and is weakly supported by Pretheoretical Fairness, it doesn't take into account the motivations and cases that tell against OIC. Denying OIC will likely make certain moral calculations more complicated. It will probably also mean that some of our intuitions are wrong. But such a theory is positioned to provide a better explanation on the whole.

The OIC defender may dig in here and say that OIC still provides the best explanation of the data, even once we take everything else into account. For all I've said so far, this may be true, but it's worth noting that, even if that were so, the explanation offered by OIC would not be as compelling or as excellent as it seemed to be when it was initially presented. What's clearly needed is a better explanation. Denying OIC doesn't help explain the present cases, and so doesn't yet explain the full range of OIC-relevant data. (After all, it's one thing to deny geocentrism and another to advance heliocentrism.) And while I don't promise to have the full explanation here, the rest of the chapter will be devoted to making a start on one.

6. Toward a Better Explanation

In this section, I will present a twofold strategy for the OIC denier. First, the OIC denier can offer a partially deflationary theory of blameworthiness and moral responsibility to capture many intuitions that seem to favor OIC. Second, the OIC denier can offer a plausible restriction on unfulfillable oughts without denying their possibility wholesale. I'll present my favored

Toward a Better Explanation   69

versions of such principles, but a full defense of them is beyond this book. Rather, this discussion aims to illustrate the general strategy in the form of a particular (and I think promising) path it might take.

The blurring of our intuitions about moral oughts and blameworthiness has come up repeatedly. I have argued that many considerations that seem to support OIC instead support a principle about blameworthiness. For example, considerations of fairness usually support a principle concerning moral responsibility and perhaps derivatively, a principle concerning our actual blaming and punishing practices. Once we take this into account, the support that remains for OIC itself is rather weak. Furthermore, it's often our epistemic condition rather than our actual abilities that factor in OIC intuitions. And our epistemic condition is intimately connected to our moral responsibility, whereas whether it is so tightly tied to our obligations is much disputed. This points to a pair of principles that replace obligation talk with moral responsibility, and ability with something epistemically bounded.

Blameworthiness Implies Intent:

> If S is blameworthy for (not) Aing, then S's (not) Aing was intentional, or S is culpably ignorant of some relevant fact.

Rational Intending:

> If S is rational, then if S does A intentionally, S must lack the belief that she cannot A.

Blameworthiness Implies Intent provides a bridge between moral responsibility and our epistemic states, and Rational Intending fleshes out those epistemic states. Both principles present minimal conditions and are not meant as full characterizations of blameworthiness or rational intentional action. The former states that, if someone is blameworthy for an action A, then either they did it intentionally or they were ignorant of some relevant fact – for example, that what the agent did was in fact A, that Aing is wrong, or that Aing causes harm. The latter states that a rational person who does A intentionally must lack the belief that she cannot A. This is consistent with the plausible thought that she must (also) have the belief that she can A. It is even consistent with the stronger thought that she must believe that she will A. But these are all further, stronger commitments, and if the present view is to be maximally accommodating, it's best to remain agnostic on these points.

These principles capture many of our OIC-supporting intuitions without making any claims about what we can actually do. Rational Intending explains the emphasis that arguments defending OIC place on what it's appropriate to say or think that we ought to do. It often makes no sense to advise someone to do something that is beyond their abilities because one cannot intend to do things that one acknowledges one cannot do. One also cannot deliberatively settle on something that one takes oneself to be unable to do. (This can be true despite the fact that it often makes plenty of sense to take into account things that one ought to do, but cannot do, in deciding what to do next.) The combination of Rational Intending with Blameworthiness Implies Intent captures one central aspect of the fairness motivation. In the previous chapter, we saw that an important reading of Unfair Demands was connected to blameworthiness rather than 'ought', and so it motivates principles along the present lines, rather than OIC.

If we add further substantive but plausible normative ethical principles, then we can capture even more of our OIC-supporting intuitions. For example, we could capture some of what seems attractive about Unfair Demands and Moral OIC, and even some of the appeal of Pretheoretical Fairness, by adding two more principles: (1) that blameworthiness for an act is inversely proportional to how demanding it is (perhaps with excessively demanding acts absolving blame entirely), and (2) that someone's lack of blameworthiness for an act makes it unfair or morally wrong, other things equal, for someone else to blame or punish them for it.

The general strategy of refocusing on blameworthiness is familiar to OIC deniers. All I have done here is to motivate and flesh out one concrete way this strategy might go. However, in adopting this strategy, the OIC denier frequently ignores the strength of the best explanation cases and remains silent on whether our oughts are restricted in any way. But surely they are restricted somehow. This is the force of the No Absurd Oughts problem. I think there's a way to resolve this problem, but it cannot remain neutral about questions in normative moral theory.

Notice first that the finger snapping and distant drowning examples don't tell the entire story. They do indeed support Standard OIC. But there are strikingly similar cases that remove the moral element. If, for example, your friend is very thirsty, you might judge that she ought to have a glass of water. You might even advise her to do so. But you're very unlikely to judge or advise that if there's no water available. To push the case even further, you wouldn't think that what she really ought to do is travel back in time so that she could have been prepared with some extra water. There's an OIC-like principle at play here that doesn't involve anything moral at all. Once we take cases like this into consideration, the best explanation will more closely resemble the version of OIC that uses the all-things-considered ought or some more inclusive practical ought.

With that in mind, it seems like what we want is a principle that will both accommodate No Absurd Oughts cases and allow some violations of OIC, and that does so in a way that extends beyond moral oughts. I'll present and provisionally defend another pair of principles that I am quite sympathetic to, but their primary function is to continue to flesh out the OIC denial strategy.

Natural Ought Principle:

If S naturally ought to A, then S can A.

Non-Natural Ought Principle:

It is not the case that, if S non-naturally ought to A, then S can A.

The Natural and Non-Natural Ought Principles need some clarification. But the main strategy is to accept the Natural Ought Principle and deny that any other form of OIC holds by maintaining the Non-Natural Ought Principle.

For the Natural and Non-Natural Ought Principles, I am drawing on the existing conception of natural duties in moral and political philosophy. A. John Simmons, for example, defines natural duties as "moral requirements which apply to all men irrespective of status or acts performed. Examples are the duty to help those in need, the duty of justice . . . , and duties of non-maleficence and respect."[20] For example, we have natural obligations (or duties or requirements) to save someone drowning nearby and not to harm passersby on the sidewalk. Let's call any other moral obligations we have non-natural. Natural obligations are not meant to contrast with artificial or fake obligations, but with constructed or created ones. Simmons and others, for example, typically contrast natural obligations with positional or institutional obligations, which I earlier collected under the umbrella heading of role obligations. Furthermore, non-natural obligations need not be voluntarily entered into. Many roles are ones that we don't voluntarily undertake, but that nevertheless come with obligations: citizen of a country, say, or certain familial and social roles.

Though I am adopting the term "natural" from this literature, I intend natural and non-natural oughts to extend beyond the original distinction in two ways. Natural and non-natural oughts in my sense both extend beyond the moral domain and extend beyond strict notions of requirement, obligation, and duty. First, we have both natural and non-natural *non-moral* oughts. Plausibly, you naturally ought to exercise, but because it's good for you, not because morality says so. And you non-naturally ought to obey the rules of a club you belong to and the laws of a country you're in. Such rules or laws may have moral implications, but it's certainly not conceptually necessary that we morally ought to obey the laws of our land. Second, it can be true that you naturally or non-naturally *ought* to do something even if you aren't *obligated* to do so. Again, it's plausible that you naturally ought to exercise, take steps to fulfill your desires, pursue knowledge, or engage in creative endeavors, without any of these things being obligatory.

As a rough pass, then, we can think of natural oughts as those things that we ought to do in virtue of the mere fact that we or others are human beings (or rational creatures, creatures capable of suffering, etc.). Non-natural oughts are all of the oughts that are not natural. These will be oughts that bear on us in virtue of some further fact – perhaps a role we have, a promise we have made, or a certain interpersonal relationship or history.

The Natural Ought Principle departs from Standard OIC in restricting it to natural oughts, but also in expanding it to include both non-moral and non-obligating oughts. So, according to the Natural Ought Principle, the fact that someone naturally ought to perform some action entails that they are both able and have the opportunity to do it. And the Non-Natural Ought Principle says that the corresponding relationship does not hold for non-natural oughts.

The Natural and Non-Natural Ought Principles very neatly capture the central counterexamples like promises and unpaid debts, since these are all non-natural oughts, and therefore able to persist in the face of inability. They can similarly accommodate many moral dilemmas, which involve non-natural obligations like conflicting promises, as well as role obligations (and oughts) – those we have insofar as we occupy certain social roles like teacher, judge, citizen, and so forth. Meanwhile, it allows that in the finger snapping and distant drowning cases, OIC does hold, since those are plausibly natural oughts. We don't generally think that we owe it to a child to save him from drowning in virtue of the fact that he bears a special relationship to us (of, say, being our own, or known to us, or a compatriot). We think that we owe it to a child to save him from drowning because he is suffering and may die, and because suffering and death are very bad things for creatures like us.

Thinking in terms of natural and non-natural oughts gives us insight into something else important. Someone very taken with science fiction stories who believes that time travel is possible may enter into a pact with someone else to travel back in time. A mathematician who believes that she can prove Goldbach's conjecture may promise to do so to her dying mentor. By allowing non-natural obligations to exist despite inability and lack of opportunity, the Natural Oughts Principle allows that such people thereby place themselves under obligations, even if the actual world isn't compatible with their fulfillment. The supplemental account of blameworthiness implies the mathematician will be blameworthy for not proving Goldbach's conjecture only if she intends not to prove it, despite her promise. However, if she intends to prove it, and gives it her best shot, but fails because it is false, too difficult, or (maybe) would consume too much of her time and therefore detract too much from her other valuable personal projects, then she may well be blameless. But she will still fail to fulfill an obligation.[21] It's also noteworthy that, if solving Goldbach's conjecture is impossible, it is not only something she is unable to do, it is something that is nomologically, metaphysically, and logically impossible. So this is a case where someone can be obligated to do even the logically impossible.

While this presents an attractive picture, it ultimately depends on substantive normative theorizing for some of its plausibility. If, for example, most of our oughts are natural, then OIC will have comparatively broad scope. If, on the other hand, almost none of them are, then OIC will have comparatively narrow scope. Which natural and non-natural oughts we have will depend on our preferred normative theories – to include ethics, but also theories of prudence, politics, the law, and so on. The extent of our non-natural moral oughts depends on a normative ethical theory as much as the extent of our non-natural prudential oughts depends on a normative theory of prudence and the extent of our non-natural legal oughts depends on a theory of law. The cases I've given so far are easy to sort, but other cases will be far more difficult.

Take familial obligations. In one respect, they seem natural. Our blood relations aren't contractual; they are in a very obvious sense naturally connected to us. But on my account, they will more closely sit with non-natural oughts. They are not obligations that we have to just anybody, in virtue of their being fellow persons, rational agents, or seats of happiness and suffering. We have such obligations in virtue of the special relationships we share with certain other people. (This also shifts the focus from "natural" blood relations to socially and interpersonally defined groups, and so is better aligned with a more accommodating conception of families.)

If we allow that some such obligations are non-natural, we can explain a wealth of other OIC violations. Take those moral dilemmas that involve rival duties to different parties, as when the obligation to tell one friend information that will benefit her conflicts with the duty to keep another friend's secret, or when duties to those close to us conflict with the impersonal duties of justice. These come out as genuinely dilemmatic. But our apparent obligations to two people drowning in opposite directions, only one of whom can be saved, will look on most moral theories like natural obligations – ones we seem to have just to other persons, regardless of our relationship to them. Thus, on the present view, such a case will not typically present a genuine moral dilemma. Instead, there will be a disjunctive obligation to save one or the other. However, if the person in question is a lifeguard, and (suppose) has sworn an oath not to let *anybody* drown on her watch, then she may well fail to do all she ought if one of the two drowns.

To take another dilemma, too, consider the mother from *Sophie's Choice*. If we allow that non-natural obligations need not be constrained by ability and opportunity, then we can explain why, assuming that she *as a mother* is obligated to keep each of her children from harm, she faces a genuine moral dilemma. It is because she has two (tragically) jointly unsatisfiable non-natural obligations, one to each child.[22]

This strikes me as a plausible outcome in both respects, in that it limits but doesn't completely eschew the existence of moral dilemmas. This approach to non-natural obligations will even help us make inroads on the most compelling complex action cases. When and why should we not steal? When and because the institutions of private property prohibit it. When and why should we apologize to people? When and because we have already wronged or harmed them and therefore exist with them in a special relationship. Lastly, because this strategy does so much to decouple moral obligation and ought from blameworthiness, it may even speak to worries about the Principle of Alternate Possibilities. Recall the concern that OIC entails the Principle of Alternate Possibilities, which many want to reject in light of Frankfurt cases (Chapter 2, Section 2.9). In non-natural ought cases, the OIC premise will be false. In natural ought cases, the present account makes denying the other premise, the conceptual connection between blameworthiness and ought, look like a more fruitful path than it did before. Admittedly, these are only suggestive remarks. Certainly more needs to be said to provide a full defense of this response, but I hope the path we would proceed along is clear enough.

I am not proposing a full account of when we are subject to natural and non-natural oughts. I am not avoiding this for space, but because the extent of our natural and non-natural oughts will depend on our normative theories, and it is no part of my project to defend particular normative theories. The case of familial obligations represents one of the several gray areas that a substantive moral theory will help adjudicate, cases where it becomes especially important to lean on a normative theory. So, for example, according to an extreme form of ethics of care, we will have moral obligations *only* to those to whom we bear some personal relationship.[23] According to an extreme form of utilitarianism, however, we have no special moral obligations that derive from our relationships. Indeed, according to an extreme form of maximizing act utilitarianism, there will be no non-natural obligations at all. Such a view won't accept, for example, that promises generate obligations. If such a view is right, then it is trivially compatible with my account here, though in combination they entail that there are no OIC violations. I disagree with that conclusion, and so I think that such a strong form of utilitarianism is wrong. (In fact, I think it's wrong for a number of other reasons as well.) Still, it is a strength of the current account of OIC that it can explain why an extreme ethics of care may contain a lot of counter-examples to Standard OIC, while extreme utilitarianism will reject them: the former theory endorses exclusively non-natural oughts, while the latter doesn't even countenance them.

For one very wedded to OIC, the foregoing remarks imply one way of holding on to Standard OIC in the moral realm, and that is to deny that there are such things as non-natural obligations. This makes OIC compatible with everything I've said in this section. So why not take this route? Aside from the fact that it allows us to hold onto OIC, there isn't much to be said for it. It's difficult to deny the existence of non-natural obligations, and the view as a whole yields a remarkable degree of explanatory power. Furthermore, by allowing OIC to hold in a restricted domain via something like the Natural Ought Principle, the view cedes OIC defenders a great deal of territory, but also allows OIC deniers to stand their ground. It is even compatible with Pretheoretical Fairness, since it limits the degree to which morality makes unsatisfiable demands.

It's the best explanation motivation that most powerfully motivates OIC, and the challenge to the OIC denier was to offer a better explanation. My position can thus be summed up by this: I have offered a better explanation. It undeniably captures much more of the moral data. Perhaps it looks like a worse explanation because it is not especially parsimonious. I've offered four major principles, and suggested an additional two to capture yet more intuitive data, and six principles for one may look like a terrible trade. In response, I want to point out that the present view relies on a lot of concepts that a full philosophical framework, if not a theory of OIC, will almost certainly provide. Any full ethical theory, for example, will have to have *some* account of blameworthiness. And some of the major assumptions I have made I take to be exceedingly lightweight (as, for example, with Rational Intending).

Notice, too, that no single version of OIC could ever have explained all of the data that have been thrust upon it. For instance, Standard OIC simply doesn't provide a theory of blameworthiness, but it has been saddled with explaining many blameworthiness-concerning intuitions. It also says nothing concerning our epistemic situation, but has been saddled with explaining situations where we must act without full information. This is, I believe, the primary reason there are so many versions of OIC on offer: each is meant to explain a slightly different set of data. So if it seems like I am invoking too many different principles, notice that the OIC defender would also have to invoke a number of principles to fully explain all of the data too.

There are, of course, kinks to be worked out, and I have only offered suggestions for how to resolve all of the issues we've looked at. Many of the concrete answers will depend on particular verdicts we reach in normative ethics, as well as other normative domains, theories of action, and theories of 'ought'. But OIC is sometimes discussed in a way that's detached from these questions. I have argued that, on the contrary, these issues are likely to be ultimately inseparable from our verdict on the principle.

Lastly, one may wonder whether my view counts as an error theory or rather a form of revisionism about OIC. I suppose that depends on what one takes to be essential to OIC, and I am not particularly interested in answering that question. I am instead offering something I take to be a good deal more powerful and interesting: a way to capture the intuitions that led us to adopt OIC in the first place, while avoiding those that undermine it.

Notes

1 Copp 2008, 71. See similar remarks in Copp 2003, 273–274.
2 Ibid., 71.
3 For example, Sapontzis writes, "what is objectionable about saying that someone is still under an obligation to do A, . . . is that saying this is pointless" (1991, 388). See also Stern: "It seems pointless to issue an order that cannot be followed" (2016, 102).
4 Cooper, e.g., defends a presupposition version of OIC, writing that "any moral 'ought'-judgment is pointless or irrational if it is impossible for the addressee to perform what it prescribes," thinking it important enough to dub Meta-Moral Principle A (1966, 49).
5 Though he dislikes this line of argument, J.W. Smith says, "Some philosophers have in their minds that in establishing 'ought implies can' they are establishing that such advice [that runs counter to OIC] makes no sense" (1961, 375).
6 Forrester (1989) defends the view that ought conversationally implicates can. He defends this view in part by noting that a god who makes unfulfillable commands has behavior that is "peculiarly pointless" (32), while also claiming that such a god "is certainly worthy of moral condemnation" (32). Forrester thus also defends Moral OIC, pointing out that "pragmatic principles may also serve as important substantive moral rules" (33). Kühler (2012) blends the two, arguing that "a *normative* principle can be formulated that (at least) blameworthiness or guilt, if to be assigned in a fair manner, *normatively* presuppose 'can'" (207).
7 Stocker calls attention to this worry, writing that "until the connection between the point of expressing a judgment and its truth is established, this . . . objection appears irrelevant" (1971, 312). Sinnott-Armstrong argues, too:

> Saying that agents ought to do what they cannot do is often claimed to be pointless and therefore not true. This argument is not valid. The premise concerns the *point* or *purpose* of saying something, but the conclusion concerns the *truth* of what is said.
>
> (1984, 251)

8 Saka 2000, 101.
9 Stern 2016, 103.
10 Jay 2013, 384.
11 It isn't too hard to think of similar cases that count against pointlessness as a motivation for OICA.

12 Compare Hill 2002, who calls situations where morality fails to guide action 'gaps', but argues that we should only presumptively disfavor gaps in a moral theory (183).
13 More precisely, this should be restricted to all morally loaded actions or all morally non-equivalent actions. Otherwise the definition is obviously too strong. For some actions, e.g., buying this soup can rather than the one directly to its left, a moral theory need not pick sides.
14 Compare Talbot 2016, who also rejects an overly narrow conception of action-guidingness used to motivate OIC.
15 Heuer 2010 talks in terms of reasons rather than oughts, but the idea is easily adapted. Stocker 1971 contains a related discussion.
16 For an argument that action-guidingness better supports denying OIC than accepting it, see Talbot 2016.
17 This example, and this way of setting up the problem, comes from Graham 2011, 372ff.
18 Some instead use the term 'crazy reasons'. See Streumer 2007, Littlejohn 2009.
19 Howard-Snyder 2004 presents a few other motivations that may be seen as related to or exploring some important species of this third category.
20 See Simmons 1979, 13. For more on natural duties, see e.g., Hart 1958, Rawls 1999, Darwall 2009, and Gilbert forthcoming. Natural duties are also related to what are sometimes called general obligations.
21 Compare an example from Smith (1961) about a student who suffers an injury on the way to a meeting with a professor (367). Smith argues that we don't hold the student to the obligation because it would be unreasonable to expect him to make the meeting, even if strictly speaking he can make it. On the view I'm presenting, we could maintain that the student fails to fulfill his obligation to make the meeting, but is obviously blameless for doing so because it would be so difficult and costly to make it.
22 We might also explain what happens in her case not as a moral dilemma, but as a different failure to do all she morally ought to do. If, rather than one obligation to each child, she has only the obligation to keep *all* of her children from harm, then the tragedy is that she ought to but cannot do *that*.
23 For such a view, see Noddings 1986.

5 Implications and Applications

1. Approach

There are two ways to approach the connection between abstract philosophical positions on the one hand and public debates and commonsense thought on the other. One attempts to underscore that nothing (or virtually nothing) of practical import follows from abstract philosophical positions. Many abstract philosophical arguments take no stance, and are careful not to commit to any stance, on issues like law, policy, punishment, and social practices. Issues like these are made messier by the presence of all sorts of factors, and one often hears that addressing the merely superficially related public debates would be a completely different project. An alternative approach acknowledges that much commonsense thought and many public debates share the spirit of the abstract philosophical arguments. This approach sees public debates as things that can be helpfully informed by a bit more careful philosophical thinking, using the very tools offered by the associated philosophical debates. It may see the abstract philosophical positions as an outgrowth of these debates, and an attempt to clarify them in productive ways – perhaps even with the thought that this is a condition of their overall success.

OIC provides a particularly interesting case, since OIC-like arguments appear constantly in public discourse and commonsense thought. As an advocate of the latter approach (at least in this case), I think it is worthwhile to see how far the previous four chapters can get us in these debates. Has our abstract philosophical stance on OIC gotten us so far from the germ of those thoughts that it no longer has anything to offer? That would be a shame. Fortunately, it's not true.

This chapter examines the debates that most saliently intersect with OIC, and the ways in which the previous chapters helpfully illuminate them. Where it may have seemed that we needed OIC to support our commonsense intuitions, I'll argue that that's not the case (or that the limited sense in which we do need it is captured by the Natural Oughts Principle). In fact, in some cases a focus on OIC distracts from the truly important questions at hand.

2. Religious Thought

We have explored Christian religious thought throughout, but we can collect these thoughts here. We saw Christian theologians who argued that God cannot command the impossible. We examined the view that morality cannot be unfair unless there is a celestial boss dictating it. And we saw the position that the inevitable failure to fulfill our obligations can promote moral humility and need not fail to guide action.

In light of the view I offered in the previous chapter, we can flesh out this picture. A celestial boss can command the impossible. Such commands will plausibly give rise to non-natural obligations because they will exist in relation to (or even because of) such commands. These commands will be, in a sense, speech acts that generate the corresponding obligations, at least on a divine command theory. So, in the same way that we can write impossible-to-fulfill obligations into contracts or make impossible-to-fulfill promises, a celestial boss can very well command us to do things we cannot do. There's no need to jump through hoops to avoid this conclusion.[1]

Plus, by distinguishing between moral wrongdoing on one hand and blameworthiness and punishment on the other, the OIC denier is free to say that such wrongdoing isn't necessarily blameworthy and doesn't necessarily deserve punishment. For the denier, determining whether such actions are blameworthy or deserve punishment will be best left to independent theories of moral responsibility and punishment.

3. Determinism, Global and Local

While determinism itself is not a frequent theme of public debate, issues related to it very much are. In this section, we'll start by examining determinism in light of the previous chapter. Getting a foundational understanding of the abstract issues will better position us to then move on to more practical ones, including disabilities, addictions, and compulsions.

3.1 Determinism and Free Will

We've already touched on the connection between OIC, free will, and determinism. If OIC is true, and determinism is true, then we never ought to do anything that we do not in fact do, because we never can do anything other than what we in fact do. This is a shocking conclusion. But there are a few different ways to avoid it. First, we can deny determinism.[2] Then, we can happily accept OIC. But those less certain about determinism can instead deny OIC. If we deny OIC, there's no problem at all. We still morally ought to do some things that we do not (and therefore cannot) do.[3]

On the view I have suggested, this may be true if the oughts in question are non-natural. If one makes a promise to do something, then even in a deterministic universe one will be obligated to fulfill that promise, even if one does not in fact fulfill the promise. However, my view, combined with determinism, will imply that all natural oughts are bound by what we can do, i.e., by what we in fact do.

This solution may seem to concede too much to the determinist by restricting the scope of our moral obligations to only non-natural obligations. This, it seems to me, is simply the cost of determinism, and may be reason to reject the view. But if we bear in mind the distinction between actions that we ought to perform and actions that we are blameworthy for or morally responsible for, then perhaps we can regain much of the seemingly lost territory. Those engaged in discussions about determinism should be concerned to capture intuitions about what we ought to do as well as what we are morally responsible for. While denying OIC as such has no implications for blameworthiness, my suggested account entails a limited form of compatibilism via the Blameworthiness Implies Intent principle. This principle offers but one piece of a full picture of moral responsibility. It allows us to hold someone morally responsible for something as long as they acted intentionally (barring culpable ignorance). Not only does this capture something very natural that underlies our blaming practices, but what's more, I think both sides of the determinism debate can get much of what they want through this principle rather than OIC.

To make the foregoing analysis more concrete, we can look at a famous deployment of determinist reasoning in Clarence Darrow's defense of Leopold and Loeb. Leopold and Loeb were friends who together murdered an acquaintance of theirs in the attempt to commit "the perfect crime." Their attempt to commit the perfect crime was unsuccessful. They were caught and eventually confessed. Though they were found guilty, Darrow presented a lengthy and impassioned argument that they should not receive the death penalty. Throughout the defense, he attempts to secure the truth of determinism.

> Science has been at work, humanity has been at work, scholarship has been at work, and intelligent people now know that every human being is the product of the endless heredity back of him and the infinite environment around him.

Then he argues from determinism to blamelessness.

> Is Dickey Loeb to blame because out of the infinite forces that conspired to form him, the infinite forces that were at work producing him ages before he was born, that because out of these infinite combinations

he was born without [an emotional life]? . . . Is he to blame that his machine is imperfect?[4]

At no time during the speech does Darrow suggest that Leopold and Loeb are innocent of the crime. That they are guilty is granted. He takes issue, however, with the question of blame and punishment. He argues that the truth of determinism entails that they lack moral responsibility for what they've done. In a nutshell, he defends a form of incompatibilism on which determinism precludes, not obligations to do what we do not in fact do, but moral responsibility, blameworthiness, and justified punishment.

Darrow argues on these grounds that it would be unfair and barbaric to give Leopold and Loeb the death penalty. Because his concern is to obtain a life imprisonment sentence instead of the death penalty, he doesn't question the justification or fairness of the former, though that would also follow from his incompatibilism. And while some will agree that they don't deserve the death penalty, the idea that *any* punishment would be unwarranted clashes fiercely with commonsense thought.

To return to the issue at hand, the OIC denier can accept that the pair have done something wrong. The OIC denier can also, using supplementary principles, hold them blameworthy even if determinism is true. In my view, Blameworthiness Implies Intent does this. In order to attribute moral responsibility or blameworthiness, we at least need to establish that the action was performed intentionally (or under culpable ignorance). And certainly Leopold and Loeb meet this criterion. Of course not every action performed intentionally will also be one for which the agent is blameworthy. But intentionality makes the action eligible for blameworthiness. In order to render the pair blameworthy, we must add a full account of moral responsibility to Blameworthiness Implies Intent. And doing so is perfectly open to the OIC denier. So although I'm not defending determinism, it's worth examining the way that someone sympathetic to determinism could approach OIC and moral responsibility. No stance on the traditional compatibilism debate follows from the denial of OIC itself, but I have offered what I take to be the best way for the OIC denier to capture our common views about moral responsibility.

3.2 Physical Disabilities

Determinism is sometimes defined as the position that, given a full description of the world at any instant together with the physical laws, one could in principle work out all of the preceding and succeeding events. If we think of this as global determinism, we can see more localized forms of determinism crop up all over. The fact that humans cannot fly unaided we might think of in this way. Given a full description of humans together with the physical laws, we can deduce that humans cannot fly unaided. If I cannot do push-ups right now because my hands are tied behind my back, then perhaps we have a very localized determinism; similarly if I am subject to a gripping compulsion. In such cases, circumstances beyond our control make it the case that certain actions are outside our reach. Indeed, many cases that are meant to lend support to OIC rely on what we might think of as localized forms of determinism. The rest of this section examines a few categories of localized determinism that are of particular philosophical and public interest. To be clear, it doesn't matter for the arguments that follow that we see these cases as localized determinism, but understanding them that way can help us see patterns in the ways the cases interact with OIC. We've already seen that, if OIC and determinism are both true, then we never ought to do anything that we do not in fact do. If OIC and any form of localized determinism is true, then it will be true in those localized cases that we never ought to do anything that we do not in fact do. So if OIC is true, then, for instance, if my hands are tied behind my back, I am not required to do push-ups.

One way to lend intuitive support to OIC is to point out that we don't think people with physical disabilities are obligated to do things that their disabilities prevent them from being able to do. For example, as I mentioned in the first chapter, we don't think a person with quadriplegia ought to lift heavy objects. We don't think that such a person ought to lift any objects at all, even in a situation where a non-disabled person would be obligated to do so. But if we deny OIC, what can we say about such a case? Must we say that people who are physically disabled are under these obligations? Must we say, for example, that someone with quadriplegia systematically fails to fulfill many more obligations than someone who lacks it? Such a conclusion seems reprehensible.

Though I find this line of thought compelling, some empirical studies suggest that people are not as quick to agree. When asked, many maintain that someone on the shore of a pond who is paralyzed (temporarily or from birth) is still morally obligated to save someone who is drowning. However, people were highly reluctant to ascribe any blame in such scenarios.[5] While the empirical studies are contested, the view I've proposed gives us an intermediate answer: A physically paralyzed person is sometimes under this obligation, but sometimes isn't. If, for example, the paralyzed person thought she would be recovered from paralysis by now and made a promise to protect the swimming person who is now drowning, then she may very well be under an obligation to swim out and save them. In fact, it seems almost patronizing to deny disabled people the power to obligate themselves in situations like these. Disabled people are the moral equals of non-disabled people, and our theory should reflect that. If, however, no non-natural obligations are involved, and she's just on the pond's edge watching this occur, then she won't be obligated to swim out and save them.

Furthermore, she won't in general be blameworthy for failing to swim out, but certain special circumstances may render her blameworthy. For example, if she has purposefully slacked at physical therapy, or doesn't realize that she cannot actually swim, but intentionally elects to remain on the shore, then she may be blameworthy – because her failure to swim out is intentional, either indirectly (in the former case) or directly (in the latter). The view I've defended thus offers a principled explanation of why it's sometimes true and sometimes false that inability entails lack of obligation, and why it's sometimes true and sometimes false that inability absolves blameworthiness. Of course, the details of both parts of this will depend on other views one holds in normative ethics. (If, for example, the person drowning is the child of the person on the pond's edge, this special relationship may give rise to non-natural obligations.) Finally, although this explanation maintains that those who are physically disabled are sometimes obligated to do what they cannot, it isn't reprehensible in any way for doing so. In some cases of inability, they will be obligated, in precisely the same way as anybody who is not physically disabled. But in many other cases, they will remain unobligated.

The same sort of explanation will apply in cases of mental disabilities, a hotly contested class of cases in the OIC literature. We can use the approach to physical disabilities to provide a parallel analysis of these cases. If an obligation is non-natural, then it does not entail the existence of a corresponding ability or 'can'. If it is natural, then it will. In that case, if the mental disability in question creates an inability to do something, then the person will not be obligated to do it. Finally, nothing I've said so far implies a stance on cases involving mental states. If a mental disability makes it the case that someone is unable to, for example, feel sympathy for another's suffering, it may be that we still want to blame such a person, or that we still think such a person ought to feel sympathy. My Blameworthiness Implies Intent principle concerns only actions, and there is plausibly a different blameworthiness principle that governs mental states (both affective and cognitive). What we say about such cases will therefore depend on which of those blameworthiness principles we endorse.[6]

3.3 Addiction and Compulsion

Insofar as cases of addiction and compulsion amount to genuine inability to refrain from addictive or compulsive behaviors,[7] they appear to present another class of cases we might see as locally deterministic. To repeat, if OIC and any form of localized determinism is true, then it will be true in those localized cases that we never ought to do anything that we do not in fact do. So, if OIC is true, then it will be false that the addict ought to refrain from the addictive behavior in question. For ease of exposition, this subsection will focus on addiction, but what I say also applies to psychological compulsions more generally.

Different models of addiction see them as variously biological, psychological, and social.[8] The corresponding senses in which and degrees to which one will be able to refrain from addictive behavior will vary across these different models. Can someone who suffers from an addiction in fact refrain from addictive behavior? Are addictive behaviors *performed* or just things that happen to someone (as with the involuntary tremors that accompany Parkinson's disease)? To what extent is addiction indirectly controllable? Regardless of what we say about these questions, if OIC is true, then an inability to refrain from the addictive behavior will preclude any 'ought' or obligation to do so. But if OIC is false, it's possible that an addict ought not, say, take another drink, despite an inability to refrain from doing so.

Like the thought that, if we live in a deterministic universe, still we ought to do some things that we do not in fact do, the thought that an addict really ought not continue to drink is sometimes presented as a counterexample to OIC. As with the previous subsections, on the present view it matters whether the putative 'ought' the addict has is best construed as natural or non-natural. If, for example, the addict has entered into a contract according to which certain addictive behaviors are prohibited, then the resulting obligation not to engage in that behavior is non-natural. If the addict finds herself in a role that morally forbids addictive behavior, as with joint financial dependency with another person, then the obligation not to gamble away joint savings may well be non-natural. In such cases, the obligation can persist despite inability to comply. However, if the addict apparently has only a natural obligation not to engage in the addictive behavior, then true inability (and not mere difficulty) will disqualify the obligation. That said, the full answers to these questions depend both on how addiction really works and what substantive normative theories we adopt.

The OIC denier can, as before, still hold that addicts are not blameworthy for addictive behavior, though this too will depend on her other views. For example, according to Blameworthiness Implies Intent, whether an addict is eligible to count as blameworthy will depend on whether addictive behavior counts as intentional, which in turn relies on how to best understand addiction together with an account of intentional action. The denial of OIC does not itself, however, imply that the addict is blameworthy, nor that the addict isn't blameworthy. Denying OIC is compatible with either, in no small part because adjudicating such cases is a complicated matter that touches on much more than OIC.

4. The Law

OIC is sometimes thought to be embodied in the law. *Impossibilium nulla obligatio est*, as the Latin legal maxim says. In other words, our inabilities form constraints on what the law can demand of us. If you aren't able to (not) do something, then it's false that you legally ought (or ought not) to do it.[9]

But it seems like laws can be contradictory and thus form a legal dilemma, structurally analogous to a moral dilemma, or even simply unsatisfiable in particular cases. So we get similar counterexamples to a legal OIC as to Standard OIC. These counterexamples rely on a straightforward understanding of what laws and legal obligations are. What makes one legally obligated to (not) do something is just whether there is a law, either on the books or enforced in practice, that says to (not) do it. In response, the defender of a legal OIC principle might argue that no genuine laws work this way. Whenever two laws appear to contradict, one of them is *not actually a law*. So, if a law appears to make an unsatisfiable demand, it doesn't actually apply. This response, I think, isn't especially persuasive. There are procedures in place to determine *how* to adjudicate between conflicting laws, giving certain people (and not others) the power to set precedent in such cases and so forth. Such people seem to take themselves to adjudicate between conflicting laws or adjust existing laws. The easiest way to make sense of these practices is to accept that surface description of what's going on.

Maybe a more viable way to relate OIC to the law is to defend something analogous to Moral OIC. Here, inability would form a normative constraint on what it's fair for the law to demand. Strictly speaking, laws can demand that we do things we cannot, but no *fair* law would do this. This suggests a different way to read the Latin legal maxim. Perhaps we are only legally obligated to do what an idealized – maybe fair, coherent, etc. – version of our existing laws demands. Such an approach looks very good at first glance, but it's worth examining the legal system to see how well this view fits with our actual practices.

A criminal trial typically consists of two phases, one to determine a verdict (in the American system, guilty or not guilty) and the other, conditional upon a verdict of guilt, to determine a sentence. Sentencing involves selecting from a range of punishments, from fines or restitution to imprisonment. In order to be found guilty, the accused must typically have both *mens rea* and *actus reus*: guilty mind and guilty action. *Mens rea* is a complex and scaling notion meant to capture the degree to which the action was performed intentionally or knowingly, and therefore whether it is something for which the accused is culpable. The central exception to this are strict liability laws, in which no *mens rea* is required. All that is required to be found guilty is that the act is performed. Sentencing, on the other hand, takes a variety of considerations into account, including mitigating factors such as personal stress or duress. And in either phase, the presence of a mental disorder can be a mitigating or exonerating factor.

Among strict liability laws are some drunk driving laws and, in many places, statutory rape laws. No *mens rea* is required to find someone guilty of these crimes. In these cases, the law makes a distinction between the performance of the illegal act and any sort of intentionality or ill will on the part of the accused. This is one way in which the law makes a distinction relevant to our inquiry. It very clearly separates law-breaking, the legal analog of moral wrongdoing, from intentionality and punishment, which then looks like the legal analog of blameworthiness. Whether the accused performed the action intentionally and whether the accused could have done otherwise are immaterial to determining guilt. And it is simply not clear whether demanding that people not do these things is unfair, even in cases where they are not able (or not knowingly able) to comply. However, it would seem unfair if such cases were punished uniformly, without regard to mitigating circumstances like inability or nonculpable ignorance. So far, this fits nicely with the OIC model I have suggested on which we deny OIC, but admit that some degree of intentionality is requisite for blameworthiness.

Laws that require *mens rea* to establish guilt, however, involve the act's either being in fact performed intentionally or knowingly, or being such that a reasonable person would have understood what was being done. Here the tidy line between wrongdoing and blameworthiness gets blurrier. And I expect this is one reason a legal analog of Moral OIC seems so attractive. But I think that we see here a genuine ambiguity in the law, and in commonsense thought, in the concept of 'guilt'. You are, in one sense, guilty for doing something wrong if you in fact did a wrong thing. In another sense, you're only guilty if you did it intentionally, knowingly, or willfully. The former sense is the one that can apply irrespective of our abilities, and the one that doesn't seem vulnerable to a fairness worry. The latter, guilt-as-culpability sense seems much more vulnerable.[10] After all, as we saw in the previous chapter, the fairness motivation is often more closely connected to blameworthiness than to 'ought'. It therefore makes sense that the *mens rea* principle above mirrors Blameworthiness Implies Intent, according to which a blameworthy act is one performed intentionally or under culpable ignorance. But the parallel between *mens rea* and Blameworthiness Implies Intent only makes sense if we understand guilt as involving moral responsibility, rather than mere wrongdoing.

Implications and Applications 87

This ambiguity does not impugn the legal system. This is because the law is a complex creature. It consists fundamentally in interpersonal demands, and it must be informed by empirical considerations. As we've seen, interpersonal demands are subject to a great deal more (and different) constraints than abstract moral demands. There are practical reasons to have a legal system that is flexible and in some places underdetermined. There are practical reasons not to populate the law with unsatisfiable legal demands that we know would frequently go unblamed and unpunished. And there are certain acts that we are so concerned to discourage that the mere performance of them, intent aside, is sufficient for blameworthiness and punishment. This is why, while it may provide illuminating distinctions and insights into these issues, OIC cannot fully determine what we should say about fairness and the law.

A last possible legal analog of Moral OIC is a principle regarding punishment. It does seem unfair to punish people who couldn't have done otherwise, at least on a retributivist view of punishment. But I think that, as before, what's really playing a role here is not whether the guilty party could have avoided doing what they did, but whether the guilty party is blameworthy. As with the cases above, if someone couldn't have avoided doing something, but nevertheless happily and knowingly does it, it strikes me as perfectly reasonable to hold that person blameworthy. Other considerations also suggest (retributivist) punishment tracks blameworthiness rather than ability to avoid. Punishments come in degrees, and so does blameworthiness. Intent enables both. Ill will, manifesting in the law as premeditation, increases the degree of both. Demandingness, manifesting in the law as duress, affects the degree of both. And here, we can invoke something resembling Unfair Demands to recapture some of the fairness motivation: It is unfair for agents (a judge or jury members) and institutions (the legal system) to criticize (or punish) people for what they are not blameworthy for, or criticize (or punish) them to a degree not proportional to their blameworthiness. But even with respect to punishment, other aims of the legal and punitive justice systems are relevant, as is their status as fundamentally interpersonal. So even if fairness favors this principle of punishment, other factors will necessarily be relevant to determining fair and appropriate punishment. A Moral OIC analog, even a variant concerning blame and punishment rather than 'ought', cannot be the whole story.

5. Equality and Rights

5.1 *Gay Rights*

The idea that homosexuality is a genetically determined trait has played a large role in the gay rights movement. Here we can see both the fairness motivation and something that looks like OIC sneaking in. If a particular person cannot be heterosexual, then it must be false that they ought to be heterosexual and it is unfair to demand that they be heterosexual. One way to articulate this comes from a *Newsweek* article titled "Blaming People for Being Gay Is Like Blaming Them for Being Left-Handed":

> Gay marriage opponents must argue that being gay is a choice – against all evidence, science and logic – because otherwise they have to confront this: Either God is a monster, condemning people to eternal torture for being what he made them, or the Bible . . . was not handed down by a deity.[11]

The first horn of the dilemma is the one that's of special interest to us. It argues that if being gay is not a choice, then God would be condemning people for what they could not have avoided being. God would be, in short, punishing people despite their inability to be otherwise.

We can use the tools we've developed so far to get a stronger grasp of the relevant issues. To start with, notice that this argument is about *being* a certain way, not *doing* something. But OIC concerns actions. It is roundly denied for traits, so that for the OIC defender, it may very well be true that you ought to *be* some way that you cannot *be*. Thus, while something like OIC looks to be deployed here, even the staunchest OIC defenders have grounds for hesitation. Next, the author talks in terms of punishment and blame. OIC defenders will again be cautious, since strictly speaking OIC is instead a claim about moral requirements. However, the notions of moral responsibility and the fairness and appropriateness of interpersonal demands is in the not-too-distant background of these thoughts. With this in place, we can begin to apply the lessons of the preceding two chapters, where we took a deep dive into our OIC-like intuitions about fairness, moral responsibility, and interpersonal demands.

The dialectic of the gay rights debate is a bit complicated. In order to deny equal rights to homosexual people, some have argued that homosexuality is a choice, i.e., something avoidable. In response, gay rights advocates have argued that homosexuality is not a choice, but an inborn trait. An assumption – for us, *the key assumption* – on both sides is that blame and punishment are only fair or justifiable insofar as the thing for which one is blamed or punished is avoidable. We have already looked at some very similar claims. One is the Principle of Alternate Possibilities, which we saw good reasons to reject (Chapter 2, Section 2.9). We also saw reasons to reject a family of similar principles concerning interpersonal blaming and punishment practices (Chapter 3). All of these principles are about action, but versions that concern ways that people *are* seem even more evidently false. We can and reasonably do blame people for being certain ways. We blame cruel and heartless people for being cruel and heartless, even if we think they can't help it. And we socially shame and even punish such people for their heartless attitudes and for any resulting actions. So the key assumption is not a firm foundation on which either side should rest its argument.

In fact, the focus on choice and avoidability threatens to undermine the strength of arguments in support of gay rights. The psychologist Lisa Diamond, known for her influential work on sexual fluidity, has been an outspoken critic of the "born this way" narrative. During one talk she said, "I feel like as a community, queers have to stop saying, 'Please help us. We were born this way and we can't change,' as an argument for legal standing. I don't think we need that argument." Instead, she says, "We can make claims for civil rights protections based on the fact that, just, you know, we are equal people, and people's rights deserve protection."[12] Actress and politician Cynthia Nixon expresses similar frustration with this narrative, captured in a *New York Times* article:

> I gave a speech recently, an empowerment speech to a gay audience, and it included the line "I've been straight and I've been gay, and gay is better." And they tried to get me to change it, because they said it implies that homosexuality can be a choice. ". . . *A certain section of our community is very concerned that it not be seen as a choice, because if it's a choice, then we could opt out.* I say it doesn't matter. . . ." Her face was red and her arms were waving. "As you can tell," she said, "I am very annoyed about this issue. Why can't it be a choice? Why is that any less legitimate? It seems we're just ceding this point to bigots who are demanding it, and I don't think that they should define the terms of the debate" (emphasis mine).[13]

As suggested by these critics, serious problems arise from resting the gay rights movement on the key assumption. If the key assumption were true, then it would end up a contingent, empirical matter whether homosexual people deserved equal rights. Why? Suppose sexual orientation turns out to be a trait that is *not* genetic or inborn and instead a matter of one's choosing. Then, per the assumption, it would be fine to deny such people rights (at least barring other reasons not to). But this isn't right. Whether people deserve equal rights is not something we need to look to science to figure out.[14]

Even more troubling is the tacit implication that homosexuality is not choiceworthy, that it is something that we would have reason to change if we could. Only because it can't be changed, we must resign ourselves to acceptance and tolerance. But this isn't right either. The reason we should accord equal rights to people of different sexual orientations is that there are significant and substantive moral reasons to do so. It has nothing to do with the (in)ability to be otherwise, and everything to do with the fact that sexual orientation is insufficient grounds for being accorded unequal rights.

5.2 Affirmative Action

Compare a related issue concerning equal treatment of different races and genders. Here, as with gay rights, the idea is that people shouldn't be punished or otherwise treated differently on the basis of features they couldn't have avoided having. This version also concerns ways that people are rather than actions, and punishment and other practices rather than any moral requirement. It therefore doesn't fall under the purview of the Standard OIC principle. Nevertheless, as above, something like OIC is at work, namely, *the key assumption*: blame and punishment are only fair or justifiable insofar as the thing for which one is blamed or punished is avoidable.

Also, as before, this assumption is used in different ways. It is sometimes associated with an anti-racist or anti-sexist perspective. Women should not be blamed or punished for being women. People of color should not be blamed or punished for not being white. These people couldn't have been otherwise, so we shouldn't punish them for these features, as racist and sexist policies do. However, the assumption is also associated with views according to which, for example, a policy like affirmative action is morally wrong. By giving more assistance to minorities, it is sometimes argued, such policies treat people differently on the basis of features that weren't chosen, features that couldn't have been otherwise. This is sometimes cast in terms of punishing those who are not minorities, sometimes simply in terms of differential rights or treatment. Here too the argument suggests a sibling of the key assumption: We shouldn't treat people differently or accord people different rights (whether positively or negatively) on the basis of features they couldn't have avoided having.[15]

We can see the same problems here. It again turns out to be an empirical matter whether people of different races and genders deserve equal rights. When concerned with disqualifying blame and punishment, it also carries the further, tacit implication that being a woman or being a person of color is not choiceworthy. It suggests that, if a person of color could choose to be white, that would be preferable (why else would blame or punishment be any question at all?). It suggests that, if a woman could choose to be a man, that would be preferable. But because it can't be changed, we must resign ourselves to acceptance and tolerance. Even when we are concerned merely with differential treatment and not blame or punishment, this line of reasoning suggests that *if* it were the sort of thing that could have been chosen, *if* it were the sort of thing that could have been otherwise, then there would be sufficient grounds for unequal treatment and rights. This kind of worry is particularly salient now. People may choose to undergo hormone replacement therapy or sex reassignment surgery. People may choose to identify as a different gender than they were assigned at birth.[16] But surely this does not license sexism or gender-based discrimination. Clearly one's ability or inability to choose which sex or gender to present as should not be a fulcrum of the debate.

The reason we should accord equal rights to people of different races and genders is because there are significant and substantive moral reasons to do so. It has, as before, nothing to do with the (in)ability to be otherwise. To point the finger at any cousin principle of OIC is to distract from the real, nonnegotiable moral territory. In the concrete case of affirmative action, we should focus on what makes it an issue of real moral concern. We should ask difficult questions about past and current inequality, reparations, the point of our social and legal institutions, and so on. Perhaps affirmative action and other color- or gender-conscious policies, even construed as unequal rights or treatment, are justified against a background of other inequalities. But it is substantive moral inquiry that will answer this question, not something like OIC.

In both the gay rights and affirmative action positions I critique, there are echoes of luck egalitarianism. This view holds that justice requires us to do away with all inequalities that are traceable to luck, including involuntary disadvantage and other factors people cannot control. So, to the extent that being gay, being a woman, or being non-white are factors that individuals cannot control that lead to inequality, political institutions are responsible for remedying those inequalities (for instance, through a redistribution of resources or through targeted policies and laws).

The view I have defended has the upshot that sometimes individuals ought to do things that they cannot do, and that sometimes individuals ought to be ways that they cannot be (even the intractably cruel person ought to be kind). So it may seem like my position is inconsistent with luck egalitarianism. However, luck egalitarianism doesn't entail OIC. In fact, the luck egalitarian can deny OIC while maintaining the key assumption or its sibling principle that we – more specifically, *political institutions* – shouldn't treat people differently on the basis of features they couldn't have avoided having, those that they have as a matter of sheer luck.

For my part, I have tried to complicate our view of the key assumption and its sibling principle. I have been at pains to distinguish what we morally ought to do, what we are morally blameworthy for, and what interpersonal and political demands are fair and unfair. We may be licensed in punishing or blaming people if they acted with ill will or malicious intent, even if they couldn't have avoided doing the thing that they in fact did (as with Frankfurt cases). There may even be times when our political institutions should blame or punish people for doing things they ought not to have done, even when those actions result from traits they happen, by matter of pure chance, to have (as with strict liability). And neither need track our moral obligations.[17]

6. Ought implies Feasible

Another variation of OIC appears in a lot of commonsense thought, one where 'ought' implies 'feasible' (OIF). Though feasibility has taken on technical meanings in the OIC debate, that's not what I mean here. There, an action is feasible when someone is sufficiently likely to succeed at it if they try, or when they can bring themselves to do it.[18] But everyday uses of OIC-like principles often involve a different sort of feasibility. An action (or outcome) is feasible when it is not excessively impractical, not too difficult, and maybe even not too personally costly. This version appears commonly in debates in political philosophy and commonsense thought about policy, and in it we can start to see reflections of the demandingness discussion from Chapter 3.

Sometimes, admittedly, these debates just rely on Standard OIC. Maybe it's false that we ought to assist those in need (to a certain degree) because we are not able to (to that degree). Onora O'Neill writes, for example, that "institutions and individuals can have obligations if but only if they have adequate capabilities to fulfill or discharge those obligations," and subsequently, "individuals cannot be obliged to resolve the problems of world hunger, or to grow wings and fly; institutions cannot have obligations to perform tasks for which they lack capabilities."[19]

But most of the time, it's not quite that. We can see this in another of O'Neill's works, where she and Neil Manson argue against the Declaration of Helsinki. The declaration outlines ethics requirements for human experimentation, including requirements governing the consent of research subjects. It requires that the subjects give explicit, preferably written consent that is *informed* and concerns *specific* research projects in which the data would be used. They seem to argue against these requirements in two ways. First, they point out that the requirements are sometimes strictly impossible to follow, and thus violate Standard OIC. However, they also argue against the requirements on the basis of their infeasibility: "Asking research subjects to grasp this complex of scientific and institutional information is highly demanding, even in the 'best' case where highly competent research subjects are recruited for prospective study."[20] In other words, because satisfying these demands isn't feasible, it isn't true that we ought to satisfy them. This is OIF.

Similar arguments take on universal health care, gun control, or drug laws. Universal health care isn't feasible because it would create too great a drain on limited resources. Stricter gun control laws or certain drug prohibitions aren't feasibly enforceable. Such arguments don't assume that these things are impossible, strictly speaking. They might well grant that the government has the financial resources to enact universal health care, but maintain that it would take too great a bite out of limited financial resources. They might well grant that we could enforce stricter gun control or drug prohibitions. We could, strictly speaking, increase the magnitude of the police force, judicial system, and prison system to enforce any violations. But doing so would force us to give up too much else. It would cost too much money, labor, time, and more. Here we see demandingness resurfacing. The objection to these policies is not that they are impossible, but that they aren't feasible – that is, they are too demanding on our various resources. Depending on exactly how we understand feasibility and demandingness, OIF at the end of the day may just mean *'ought' implies not-too-demanding*.

Though these examples concern policy, OIF is ubiquitous. Should we remove value judgments from science? According to one philosopher of science, "It is virtually impossible to prevent science from being influenced by values or supporting some values over others," and therefore "scientists should consider the roles of values in their work."[21] If "virtually impossible" indicates a strong form of infeasibility without indicating strict impossibility, then we see infeasibility removing an 'ought'. Should citizens be fully informed about political issues? Even if this were possible, it's certainly infeasible. Should I grade all 150 student essays in one day? It's possible, but infeasible given my other needs and projects. So OIF says the answer to both is no.

But if OIC is false, then OIF is false too, since any case in which we ought to do something that we can't is plausibly also a case where we ought to do something that is not *feasible* in the current sense.[22] Even if OIC were true, OIF may still be false. There are plausibly all sorts of things that we ought to do that are impractical, difficult, or costly. To take an extreme case, if you see a drowning child that you could save, but you're wearing very expensive clothing, then diving in is demanding in that it is costly. Perhaps it would also be difficult for you, and even impractical (because of a very awkward slope down to the pond's edge). Still, you ought to save the child. If we can comply with the Helsinki requirements, even if it's greatly impractical, then maybe we have at least some reason to do so. Indeed, on my view, since the Helsinki requirements are non-natural obligations, neither inability nor infeasibility will disqualify the obligation to comply, though blame may well be mitigated.

94 Implications and Applications

A careful reader may notice that the above arguments often don't say that, because existing policies are infeasible, we as *citizens* aren't obligated to comply with or obey them. Rather, they aim to show that, because some policies are infeasible, *institutions* shouldn't adopt them. In this, they assume neither OIC nor OIF. OIF would have it that moral requirements and other 'oughts' are extinguished when they are infeasible. Here, by contrast, the suggestion is that the infeasibility of policies creates an unfair burden on those bound by the policy (citizens, experimenters, etc.). In fact, this suggestion fits well with a view that denies OIF: if institutions were to adopt such policies, those policies would obligate people to comply, but forcing those bound by the policies to fail to fulfill many of their obligations would be unfair to them. Indeed, it fits better with a variant of Moral OIC. Call it Moral OIF: If an action is infeasible for someone, then one (morally) ought not demand that they do it; or if one is (morally) permitted to demand that someone ought to do something, then that action is feasible for them to do. Of course, this is reminiscent of claims like Interpersonal Fairness and Unfair Demands, which in part address how fair or unfair it is to demand that people do things that are very difficult or costly. But is Moral OIF true? Does infeasibility count against policy creation?

We saw in Chapter 3 that many things govern whether it is fair or unfair to demand something of someone else, and we have seen this reappearing throughout this chapter. So too here the answer will depend on a variety of empirical and moral considerations. If adopting a policy would severely drain some resources, then we must assess the relative importance of the other ends those resources could be used for. If they're significant enough, then obviously that's a strike against adopting the resource-demanding policy. But this is just the familiar form of weighing reasons for or against something – it's nothing special about feasibility. Furthermore, it may be that having an ambitious but infeasible policy would produce better results than an existing but unambitious policy. Answering these questions involves both empirical work to determine likely outcomes, and substantive moral theory to characterize what count as better or worse results.

In the end, I don't think that infeasibility itself plays any role in determining whether a policy should be adopted. Extrinsic features of infeasibility will of course be relevant. If having an infeasible policy creates constant confusion, if it results in people being disproportionately punished for non-compliance, even if it just results in undesirable guilt and shaming practices – all of these will count against a policy. But this won't be infeasibility *itself* counting against it.

In this chapter, I have attempted to collect and even, to some extent, organize the different practical and commonsense upshots OIC is believed to have. I have in each case shown how the OIC denier, especially one who

Implications and Applications 95

takes seriously the strategy I offered in the previous chapter, can accommodate all of these cases. This has been aimed at readers who are concerned that OIC is required for various desirable and fair positions. By looking at a variety of practical cases, I've tried to give a varied sense of how, though OIC may seem like a can't-do-without-it sort of principle, one very much can do without it.

Notes

1 Of course, someone sympathetic to a Moral OIC view might concede that in one sense a celestial boss *could* issue such commands, a perfectly good god *would not* do so as it would be unfair. For more on the way that celestial bosses are related to fairness arguments, see Chapter 3, Section 2.
2 We could also endorse 'can'-compatibilism, though I don't find this very promising, for reasons discussed in Chapter 2, Section 2.8.
3 Denying OIC has the additional advantage of avoiding Saka's related worry (2000) that even the epistemic possibility of determinism undermines OIC.
4 Clarence Darrow in his Summation for the Defense, *People v. Leopold and Loeb* (1924).
5 Buckwalter and Turri 2015.
6 With respect to complex actions like thanking (that include both a behavioral and mental component), discussed in Chapter 2, Section 2.7, the present view offers two options. One is to hold that whatever we say about obligations and blameworthiness concerning mental states will apply a fortiori to these. The other is to maintain the same analysis for complex actions as for other actions: If the obligation is non-natural, then it may violate OIC. If it is natural, then it doesn't. For my part, I'm inclined toward the latter.
7 By 'addictive behavior', I mean behaviors that are caused by addiction, not behaviors that contribute to or foster addiction.
8 For an overview of the different theories, see EMCDDA (European Monitoring Centre for Drugs and Drug Addiction) and West 2013.
9 In this section, I will set aside whether laws or legal obligations give rise to moral obligations. If they do, it is open to the OIC denier to reject any legal implications that OIC is thought to have.
10 Compare the *nulla poena sine culpa* principle that appears in European criminal law: no punishment without *culpa*, which we could translate informally as 'guilt', or more carefully as 'culpability'.
11 Eichenwald 2015.
12 Diamond 2013.
13 Witchel 2012.
14 However, it may be the case that "born this way" arguments in public discourse currently do much more good than harm. My point is that, from the perspective of moral theory, it is not a firm foundation. If and when people are able to choose or change their sexual orientation, we will have to face this. See Delmas and Aas 2018 for a discussion of these issues.
15 See Boxill 1984 for more on this.
16 This sets aside a variety of complex questions, including whether people may choose to *experience* themselves as one gender rather than another.

17 Thanks to Sean Aas for pointing out this connection to luck egalitarianism.
18 See Lawford-Smith 2013 for a discussion of institutions, collectives, and OIC.
19 O'Neill 2004, 251. See Buckwalter forthcoming for more on this move.
20 Manson and O'Neill 2007, 8–9.
21 Elliott 2017, 13.
22 To repeat, I don't mean feasibility in the technical sense that the literature has adopted; in that sense, OIC's falsity does not entail OIF's falsity.

6 Conclusion

In this book, we've looked at a variety of different OIC principles. We started with Standard OIC, the principle that an agent's being morally obligated to perform some action analytically entails that that agent is able to perform it. We examined prominent variations of it, paying special attention to pragmatic and moral versions, versions that broadened the relevant notion of 'ought', and cousin blameworthiness principles.

In Chapter 2, I mentioned that there are two ways that the OIC denier typically tries to recover what is lost by rejecting OIC. One is by defending weakened, pragmatic versions of OIC, and the other is by defending slightly altered versions that substitute blameworthiness for 'ought' (or more precisely, 'ought not'). As will be evident, I favor the latter over the former. But I haven't allied myself fully with it. I have provided a different strategy, one that takes seriously motivations for OIC as well as motivations for denying OIC.

My strategy has not been to reject OIC entirely, but to restrict its sphere of influence. This was chiefly in response to the best explanation motivation. This motivation for OIC is powerful, and I think it is very hard to capture in any way other than some form of OIC. So I have offered a principled way to sort cases where OIC holds from cases where it doesn't. Because I deny that OIC always and necessarily holds, I count myself among OIC deniers, and present this book as offering a general strategy for how best to go about denying OIC. But I do not defend the view that OIC never holds. In order to capture many of the other intuitions we've discussed, I have supplemented the core view about OIC with a few other principles: one specifying a necessary condition for blameworthiness; one specifying a necessary condition for rational, intentional action; and a pair of substantive moral principles meant to capture major aspects of demandingness and fairness.

Of course, someone very taken with defending OIC is likely not to be convinced by the arguments I've presented or the view I've offered. The OIC defender may take two routes to avoid many of the problems I point out. One approach is to simply deny all of the problems raised in Chapter 2.

I haven't shown any internal inconsistency in adopting OIC, just a lot of very costly tradeoffs. Therefore the OIC defender may, without any incoherence, deny all of the claims and views that lead to conflicts with OIC. But at least it should be apparent at this point that this leaves the defender with an awful lot to deny. On the other hand, the OIC defender may look to versions of OIC that I couldn't address here. However, I think most of them, if not all, face problems that are variants of the ones we've seen for Standard OIC.

That said, I haven't been able to present any such arguments in full. Some, I haven't been able to present even in part. We must all make tradeoffs, and the method I have used here sacrifices depth for breadth. I have done this because there aren't many, if any, places where one can get a relatively detailed, organized, and tidy coverage of the enormous and diffuse literature on OIC. But it also means that there are many things that I haven't been able to spell out in detail, both in terms of objections to OIC and developments of my positive view, and I have left many questions unanswered.

Still, in assessing any view, one wants to know not only what the objections are, but why we should adopt the view in the first place. Even if all of the objections fell flat, in order to favor OIC, there would have to be some support for it. So what pushes us to adopt OIC? Mainly to explain how we very reasonably get people off the hook for certain obligations and 'oughts'. But as we've seen, we can do that in lots of ways: principles about blameworthiness, constraints on what's interpersonally fair, and a restricted OIC principle, to name some. And what's more, we don't always want to get people off the hook, even if they are unable to do what they ought to do.

Another thing I hope to have conveyed is the sheer wealth of phenomena that are commonly attributed to OIC. Phenomena surrounding moral responsibility, fairness and demandingness, semantics and pragmatics, deliberation, action theory, politics and policy, the law, and more. This is too great a burden for any one principle to shoulder, and these and more have been foisted upon OIC. Its defenders and deniers alike need at least a few different principles to explain all of this.

I have tried my very best to make this theory an honest one, in the sense that I have tried to approach the arguments without any antecedent aims, not secretly hoping that it would turn out one way rather than another. I hope that it shows, and that, even if the view turns out to be lacking in some details or simply incorrect, it pushes the OIC debate in a fruitful direction.

Don't get me wrong. In the end I quite like the theory I present. It avoids what strike me as the two most common pitfalls of going OIC views: the binary thinking that OIC must be either everywhere true or everywhere false, and the isolation of the OIC debate from other areas of philosophical inquiry. It is both suitably flexible – in that it can, for example, be allied with a variety of normative ethical theories – and suitably fleshed out to be of use to other areas of philosophy and even commonsense moral thought. And it does an impressive job capturing the staggering variety of OIC phenomena. It also captures the very human reality that, as we like to put it, life is sometimes unfair. Sometimes it is tragic. And an important part of what it is to be human is to navigate that reality with care and sensitivity rather than try to erase it.

Bibliography

Alston, William P. "The Deontological Conception of Epistemic Justification." *Philosophical Perspectives* 2 (1988): 257–299.

Arpaly, Nomy. *Merit, Meaning, and Human Bondage: An Essay on Free Will*. Princeton, NJ: Princeton University Press, 2006.

Arthur, John. "Famine Relief and the Ideal Moral Code." In *Ethics in Practice: An Anthology*, ed. Hugh LaFollette, 3rd ed., 623–632. Malden, MA: Blackwell, 2007.

Austin, John. "A Plea for Excuses." *Proceedings of the Aristotelian Society* 57 (1956): 1–30.

Benn, Claire. "Over-Demandingness Objections and Supererogation." In *The Limits of Moral Obligation: Moral Demandingness and Ought Implies Can*, ed. Marcel van Ackeren and Michael Kühler, New York: Routledge, 2016.

Berg, Amy. "Ideal Theory and 'Ought Implies Can'." *Pacific Philosophical Quarterly* 99, 4 (2018): 869–890.

Besch, Thomas M. "Factualism, Normativism and the Bounds of Normativity." *Dialogue* 50, 2 (2011): 347–365.

Bloomfield, Paul. "Two Dogmas of Metaethics." *Philosophical Studies* 132, 3 (2007): 439–466.

Blum, Alex. "The Kantian Versus Frankfurt." *Analysis* 60, 3 (2000): 287–288.

Boxill, Bernard. "The Color-Blind Principle." In *Blacks and Social Justice*, 9–18. Lanham, MD: Rowman & Littlefield Publishers, 1984.

Brandt, Richard B. *A Theory of the Good and the Right*. New York, NY: Prometheus Books, 1998.

Brown, James. "Moral Theory and the Ought – Can Principle." *Mind* 86, 342 (1977): 206–223.

Buckwalter, Wesley. "Ability, Responsibility, and Global Justice." *Journal of the Indian Council of Philosophical Research*, forthcoming.

Buckwalter, Wesley, and John Turri. "Inability and Obligation in Moral Judgment." *PLoS ONE* 10, 8 (2015).

Bykvist, Krister, and Anandi Hattiangadi. "Does Thought Imply Ought?" *Analysis* 67, 4 (2007): 277–285.

Chituc, Vladimir, Paul Henne, Walter Sinnott-Armstrong, and Felipe De Brigard. "Blame, Not Ability, Impacts Moral 'Ought' Judgments for Impossible Actions:

Toward an Empirical Refutation of 'Ought' Implies 'Can'." *Cognition* 150 (2016): 20–25.
Chuard, Philippe, and Nicholas Southwood. "Epistemic Norms Without Voluntary Control." *Noûs* 43, 4 (2009): 599–632.
Collingridge, David G. "'Ought-Implies-Can' and Hume's Rule." *Philosophy* 52, 201 (1977): 348–351.
Conee, Earl. "Against Moral Dilemmas." *Philosophical Review* 91, 1 (1982): 87–97.
Cooper, Neil. "Some Presuppositions of Moral Judgments." *Mind* 75, 297 (1966): 45–57.
Copp, David. "Defending the Principle of Alternate Possibilities: Blameworthiness and Moral Responsibility." *Noûs* 31, 4 (1997): 441–456.
———. "'Ought' Implies 'Can', Blameworthiness, and the Principle of Alternate Possibilities." In *Moral Responsibility and Alternative Possibilities: Essays on the Importance of Alternative Possibilities*, ed. David Widerker and Michael McKenna, 265–299. Burlington, VT: Ashgate, 2003.
———. "'Ought' Implies 'Can' and the Derivation of the Principle of Alternate Possibilities." *Analysis* 68, 1 (2008): 67–75.
Cullity, Garrett. "Demandingness, 'Ought', and Self-Shaping." In *The Limits of Moral Obligation: Moral Demandingness and Ought Implies Can*, ed. Marcel van Ackeren and Michael Kühler. New York: Routledge, 2016.
Dahl, Norman O. "Ought Implies Can and Deontic Logic." *Philosophia* 4, 4 (1974): 485–511.
Darrow, Clarence. *People v Leopold and Loeb*, 33623 and 33624 (Cook County Circuit Court 1924).
Darwall, Stephen. *The Second-Person Standpoint: Morality, Respect, and Accountability*. Cambridge, MA: Harvard University Press, 2009.
de la Cruz. Juana Inés. *The Answer: Including Sor Filotea's Letter and New Selected Poems = La Respuesta*, trans. Electa Arenal and Amanda Powell. New York, NY: Feminist Press at the City University of New York, 2009.
DeLapp, Kevin. *Moral Realism*. London: Bloomsbury, 2013.
Delmas, Candice, and Sean Aas. "Sexual Reorientation in Ideal and NonIdeal Theory." *Journal of Political Philosophy* 26, 4 (2018): 463–485.
Diamond, Lisa. "Just How Different Are Female and Male Sexual Orientation?" Lecture. Cornell University, October 17, 2013. www.youtube.com/watch?v=m2r THDOuUBw.
Dorsey, Dale. "Objective Morality, Subjective Morality, and the Explanatory Question." *Journal of Ethics and Social Philosophy* 6, 3 (2012).
Driver, Julia. "Promising Too Much." In *Promises and Agreements*, ed. Hanoch Sheinman, 183–197. Oxford: Oxford University Press, 2011.
Eichenwald, Kurt. "Blaming People for Being Gay Is Like Blaming Them for Being Left-Handed." *Newsweek*, May 5, 2015. www.newsweek.com/2015/05/15/gay-choice-science-homosexuality-328285.html.
Elliott, Kevin C. *A Tapestry of Values: An Introduction to Values in Science*. New York, NY: Oxford University Press, 2017.
Estlund, David. "Human Nature and the Limits (If Any) of Political Philosophy." *Philosophy and Public Affairs* 39, 3 (2011): 207–237.

Bibliography

Feldman, Richard. "Voluntary Belief and Epistemic Evaluation." In *Knowledge, Truth, and Duty: Essays on Epistemic Justification, Responsibility, and Virtue*, ed. Matthias Steup. Oxford and New York: Oxford University Press, 2001.

Fischer, John M. "'Ought-implies-can', causal determinism and moral responsibility." *Analysis* 63 (2003): 244–250.

Fintel, Kai von, and Sabine Iatridou. "How to Say Ought in Foreign: The Composition of Weak Necessity Modals." In *Time and Modality*, ed. Jacqueline Guéron and Jacqueline Lecarme, 115–141. Dordrecht: Springer Netherlands, 2008.

Forrester, James W. *Why You Should: The Pragmatics of Deontic Speech*. Hanover, NH: University Press of New England, 1989.

Frankfurt, Harry G. "Alternate Possibilities and Moral Responsibility." *Journal of Philosophy* 66, 23 (1969): 829–839.

Gilbert, Margaret. *Rights and Demands: A Foundational Inquiry*. Oxford and New York, NY: Oxford University Press, forthcoming.

Gowans, Christopher W. "Introduction: The Debate on Moral Dilemmas." In *Moral Dilemmas*, ed. Christopher W. Gowans, 3–33. New York, NY: Oxford University Press, 1987.

Graham, Peter A. "'Ought' and Ability." *Philosophical Review* 120, 3 (2011): 337–382.

Greve, Rob van Someren. "'Ought', 'Can', and Fairness." *Ethical Theory and Moral Practice* 17, 5 (2014): 913–922.

Grice, Herbert Paul. "Logic and Conversation." In *Studies in the Way of Words*, 41–58. Cambridge, MA: Harvard University Press, 1967.

Haji, Ishtiyaque. *Deontic Morality and Control*. New York, NY: Cambridge University Press, 2002.

Hampshire, Stuart. "Symposium: Freedom of the Will." *Aristotelian Society Supplementary Volume* 25, 1 (1951): 161–178.

Hardimon, Michael O. "Role Obligations." *Journal of Philosophy* 91, 7 (1994): 333–363.

Hare, Richard Mervyn. *Freedom and Reason*. Clarendon Paperbacks. Oxford: Clarendon Press, 1963.

———. "Symposium: Freedom of the Will." *Aristotelian Society Supplementary Volume* 25, 1 (1951): 201–216.

Harman, Gilbert. "Moral Relativism Defended." *The Philosophical Review* 84, 1 (1975): 3–22.

Hart, H.L.A. "Legal and Moral Obligation." In *Essays in Moral Philosophy*, ed. Abraham Irving Melden, 82–107. Seattle, WA: University of Washington Press, 1958.

Henne, Paul, Vladimir Chituc, Felipe De Brigard, and Walter Sinnott-Armstrong. "An Empirical Refutation of 'Ought' Implies 'Can'." *Analysis* 76, 3 (2016): 283–290.

Herman, Barbara. "Obligation and Performance." In *The Practice of Moral Judgment*, 159–183. Cambridge, MA: Harvard University Press, 1996.

Heuer, Ulrike. "Reasons and Impossibility." *Philosophical Studies* 147, 2 (2010): 235–246.

Hill, Thomas E. *Moral Dilemmas and Moral Theory*, ed. H. E. Mason. New York, NY: Oxford University Press, 2002.

Howard-Snyder, Frances. "'Cannot' Implies 'Not Ought'." *Philosophical Studies* 130, 2 (2004): 233–246.

———. "The Rejection of Objective Consequentialism." *Utilitas* 9, 2 (1997): 241–248.
Hume, David. *A Treatise of Human Nature*, ed. Lewis Amherst Selby-Bigge and Peter Harold Nidditch. Oxford: Clarendon Press, 1978.
Hurka, Thomas. *Virtue, Vice, and Value*. New York, NY: Oxford University Press, 2003.
Huss, Brian. "Three Challenges (and Three Replies) to the Ethics of Belief." *Synthese* 168, 2 (2009): 249–271.
Jay, Christopher. "Impossible Obligations Are Not Necessarily Deliberatively Pointless." *Proceedings of the Aristotelian Society* 113, 3 (2013): 381–389.
Kant, Immanuel. *Groundwork of the Metaphysics of Morals*, ed. Mary J. Gregor. Cambridge: Cambridge University Press, 1998.
———. "On the Common Saying: That May Be Correct in Theory, But It Is of No Use in Practice." In *Practical Philosophy*, ed. and trans. Mary J. Gregor, 273–309. Cambridge: Cambridge University Press, 1996.
Kekes, John. "'Ought Implies Can' and Two Kinds of Morality." *Philosophical Quarterly* 34, 137 (1984): 459–467.
King, Alex. "Actions That We Ought, But Can't." *Ratio* 27, 3 (2014), 316–327.
———. "The Culpable Inability Problem for Synchronic and Diachronic 'Ought Implies Can'." *Journal of Moral Philosophy* 16, 1 (2019): 50–62.
———. "'Ought Implies Can': Not So Pragmatic After All." *Philosophy and Phenomenological Research* 95, 3 (2017): 637–661.
Kramer, Matthew H. "Moral Conflicts, the 'Ought Implies Can' Principle and Moral Demandingness." In *The Limits of Moral Obligation: Moral Demandingness and Ought Implies Can*, ed. Marcel van Ackeren and Michael Kühler. New York, NY: Routledge, 2016.
———. "Moral Rights and the Limits of the Ought-Implies-Can Principle: Why Impeccable Precautions Are No Excuse." *Inquiry* 48, 4 (2005): 307–355.
Kratzer, Angelika. "Modality." In *Semantik/Semantics, Ein Internationales Handbuch Der Zeitgenössischen Forschung. An International Handbook of Contemporary Research*, ed. Arnim von Stechow and Dieter Wunderlich, 639–650. Berlin and Boston, MA: De Gruyter Mouton, 1991.
———. "What 'Must' and 'Can' Must and Can Mean." *Linguistics and Philosophy* 1, 3 (1977): 337–355.
Kühler, Michael. "Demanding the Impossible: Conceptually Misguided or Merely Unfair?" In *The Limits of Moral Obligation: Moral Demandingness and Ought Implies Can*, ed. Marcel van Ackeren and Michael Kühler. New York, NY: Routledge, 2016.
———. "Who Am I to Uphold Unrealizable Normative Claims?" In *Autonomy and the Self*, ed. Michael Kühler and Nadja Jelinek, 191–209. Dordrecht: Springer, 2012.
Kurthy, Miklos, Holly Lawford-Smith, and Paulo Sousa. "Does Ought Imply Can?" *PLoS ONE* 12, 4 (April 12, 2017): e0175206. https://doi.org/10.1371/journal.pone.0175206.
Lawford-Smith, Holly. "Non-Ideal Accessibility." *Ethical Theory and Moral Practice* 16, 3 (2013): 653–669.

———. "The Feasibility of Collectives' Actions." *Australasian Journal of Philosophy* 90, 3 (2012): 453–467.
Lemmon, Edward John. "Moral Dilemmas." *Philosophical Review* 71, 2 (1962): 139–158.
Littlejohn, Clayton. "'Ought', 'Can', and Practical Reasons." *American Philosophical Quarterly* 46, 4 (2009): 363–373.
Manson, Neil C., and Onora O'Neill. *Rethinking Informed Consent in Bioethics*. Cambridge and New York, NY: Cambridge University Press, 2007.
Martin, Wayne. "VI – Ought but Cannot." *Proceedings of the Aristotelian Society* 109 (2009): 103–128.
Marx, Karl. "Critique of the Gotha Program." In *The Marx-Engels Reader*, ed. Robert C. Tucker, 525–541. New York, NY: Norton, 1978.
McElwee, Brian. "What Is Demandingness?" In *The Limits of Moral Obligation: Moral Demandingness and Ought Implies Can*, ed. Marcel van Ackeren and Michael Kühler. New York, NY: Routledge, 2016.
McNamara, Paul. "Must I Do What I Ought (or Will the Least I Can Do Do)?" In *Deontic Logic, Agency and Normative Systems*, ed. Mark A. Brown and Jose Carmo, 154–173. London: Springer London, 1996.
Mencius. *Mencius*, ed. Phillip J. Ivanhoe, trans. Irene Bloom. New York: Columbia University Press, 2009.
Mill, John Stuart, Jeremy Bentham, and Alan Ryan. *Utilitarianism and Other Essays*. New York, NY: Penguin Books, 1987.
Mizrahi, Moti. "'Ought' does not imply 'can'." *Philosophical Frontiers* 4, 1 (2009): 19–35.
Mizrahi, Moti. "Does 'Ought' Imply 'Can' from an Epistemic Point of View?" *Philosophia* 40, 4 (2012): 829–840.
———. "Ought, Can, and Presupposition: An Experimental Study." *Methode* 4, 6 (2015): 232–243.
Moore, Michael S. "Patrolling the Borders of Consequentialist Justifications: The Scope of Agent-Relative Restrictions." *Law and Philosophy* 27, 1 (2007): 35–96.
Nagel, Thomas. *Equality and Partiality*, 1991. New York: Oxford University Press.
Nelkin, Dana Kay. "Difficulty and Degrees of Moral Praiseworthiness and Blameworthiness." *Noûs* 50, 2 (June 1, 2016): 356–378.
Noddings, Nel. *Caring: A Feminine Approach to Ethics and Moral Education*. Berkeley, CA: University of California Press, 1986.
O'Neill, Onora. "Global Justice: Whose Obligations?" In *The ethics of assistance: Morality and the Distant Needy*, ed. Deen K. Chatterjee, 242–259. Cambridge: Cambridge University Press, 2004.
Pereboom, Derk. "Determinism Al Dente." *Noûs* 29, 1 (1995): 21–45.
Rawls, John. *A Theory of Justice*. Cambridge, MA: Harvard University Press, 1999.
Rees, Brinley Roderick. *Pelagius: Life and Letters*. Rochester, NY: Boydell Press, 1998.
Ross, W.D. (Sir David). *Foundations of Ethics*. Oxford: Clarendon Press, 1963.
Saka, Paul. "Ought Does Not Imply Can." *American Philosophical Quarterly* 37, 2 (2000): 93–105.

Sapontzis, Steve F. "'Ought' Does Imply 'Can'." *Southern Journal of Philosophy* 29, 3 (1991): 382–393.
Schroeder, Mark. "Ought, Agents, and Actions." *Philosophical Review* 120, 1 (2011): 1–41.
Schwan, Ben. "What Ability Can Do." *Philosophical Studies* 175, 3 (2018): 703–723.
Sidgwick, Henry. *The Methods of Ethics*. Indianapolis: Hackett, 1981.
Simmons, John A. *Moral Principles and Political Obligations*. Princeton, NJ: Princeton University Press, 1979.
Singer, Peter. "Outsiders: Our Obligations to Those beyond Our Borders." In *The Ethics of Assistance: Morality and the Distant Needy*, ed. Deen K. Chatterjee, 11–32. Cambridge: Cambridge University Press, 2004.
Sinnott-Armstrong, Walter. *Moral Dilemmas*. Philosophical Theory. Oxford and New York, NY: Basil Blackwell, 1988.
———. "'Ought' Conversationally Implies 'Can'." *Philosophical Review* 93, 2 (1984): 249–261.
———. "'Ought to Have' and 'Could Have'." *Analysis* 45, 1 (1985): 44–48.
Sloman, Aaron. "'Ought' and 'Better'." *Mind* 79, 315 (1970): 385–394.
Smith, James Ward. "Impossibility and Morals." *Mind* 70, 279 (1961): 362–375.
Southwood, Nicholas. "Does 'Ought' Imply 'Feasible'?" *Philosophy and Public Affairs* 44, 1 (2016): 7–45.
Statman, Daniel. *Moral Dilemmas*. Amsterdam: Rodopi, 1995.
Stern, Robert. "Does 'Ought' Imply 'Can'? And Did Kant Think It Does?" *Utilitas* 16, 1 (2004): 42–61.
———. "Why Does Ought Imply Can?" In *The Limits of Moral Obligation: Moral Demandingness and Ought Implies Can*, ed. Marcel van Ackeren and Michael Kühler. New York, NY: Routledge, 2016.
Stocker, Michael. "'Ought' and 'Can'." *Australasian Journal of Philosophy* 49, 3 (1971): 303–316.
Streumer, Bart. "Reasons and Ability." In *The Oxford Handbook of Reasons and Normativity*, ed. Daniel Star. Oxford: Oxford University Press, forthcoming.
———. "Reasons and Impossibility." *Philosophical Studies* 136, 3 (2007): 351–384.
———. "Reasons, Impossibility and Efficient Steps: Reply to Heuer." *Philosophical Studies* 151, 1 (2010): 79–86.
Talbot, Brian. "The Best Argument for 'Ought Implies Can' Is a Better Argument Against 'Ought Implies Can'." *Ergo* 3 (2016).
Tessman, Lisa. *Moral Failure: On the Impossible Demands of Morality*. Oxford and New York, NY: Oxford University Press, 2014.
Vallentyne, Peter. "Two Types of Moral Dilemmas." *Erkenntnis* 30, 3 (May 1989): 301–318.
Velleman, James David. *The Possibility of Practical Reason*. Ann Arbor, MI: University of Michigan Library, 2000.
Vranas, Peter B.M. "I Ought, Therefore I Can." *Philosophical Studies* 136, 2 (2007): 167–216.
Vranas, Peter B.M. " "Ought" Implies "Can" but Does Not Imply "Must": An Asymmetry between Becoming Infeasible and Becoming Overridden." *Philosophical Review*, forthcoming.

West, Robert, and European Monitoring Centre for Drugs and Drug Addiction. *Models of Addiction*. Luxembourg: Publications Office, 2013.
Widerker, David. "Frankfurt on 'Ought Implies Can' and Alternative Possibilities." *Analysis* 51, 4 (October 1, 1991): 222–224.
Wiens, David. "Motivational Limitations on the Demands of Justice." *European Journal of Political Theory* 15, 3 (2016): 333–352.
Williams, Bernard. "A Critique of Utilitarianism." In *Utilitarianism: For and Against*, ed. J.J.C. Smart and Bernard Williams, 77–150. Cambridge, UK: Cambridge University Press, 1973.
Witchel, Alex. "Cynthia Nixon's Life After 'Sex'." *The New York Times*, January 19, 2012. www.nytimes.com/2012/01/22/magazine/cynthia-nixon-wit.html.
Yaffe, Gideon. "'Ought' Implies 'Can' and the Principle of Alternate Possibilities." *Analysis* 59, 3 (1999): 218–222.
Zimmerman, Michael J. *The Concept of Moral Obligation*. Cambridge Studies in Philosophy. Cambridge and New York, NY: Cambridge University Press, 1996.
———. "Remote Obligation." *American Philosophical Quarterly* 24, 2 (1987): 199–205.

Index

Page numbers in italic indicate a figure on the corresponding page.

ability 11–12, 18, 20, 22–23, 34, 69, 74, 82–84, 87, 90–91; degrees of 23; general 12; and knowledge 12; specific 12; *see also* culpable inability
action: as object of OIC 3, 14–15, 18–19, 23–24, 88–90; complex 31–33, 74, 95; demands as an instance 51–54; and guidance, *see* action-guidingness; intentionality of 81, 84–86, 97; moral responsibility for, *see* moral responsibility, blameworthiness; and omission, *see* omissions; remote 15–16, 21; theory of 76, 98
action-guidingness 42, 59–61, 63–66, 77, 79
addiction 10–11, 34, 83–85
advising 3, 62–63, 66, 70
affirmative action 90–92
Agential Fairness principle 46–47, 55
agents 14, 18, 46–47, 56, 87; ideal 13; *see also* Agential Fairness principle
Agglomeration Principle 29–31
Aquinas, St Thomas 1
Arpaly, Nomy 47
Austin, J.L. 27

blameworthiness 69–76, 79–92, 97–98; and demandingness 70, 72–73, 77; and determinism 33–34, 80–81; distinguished from ought and obligation 27, 69–70, 74, 79–80, 97; and excuses 27, 58; and fairness 43, 52–54, 70, 72–73; for traits 88–92; and intent 69–70, 81, 86; and law 86–87; principles regarding, 2, 37, 41, 66, 68–70, 75, 83, 97–98; and punishment 69, 80–81, 86–92; studies about 82; *see also* Blameworthiness Implies Intent principle; Principle of Alternate Possibilities
Blameworthiness Implies Intent principle 69–70, 80–81, 83–84, 86; *see also* intention
born this way 87–90, 95

can 3, 9–14; as ability and opportunity, *see* ability, opportunity; as control, *see* control; as moral permissibility, 20; as possibility, *see* possibility
Cannot Implies Not-Ought *see* Ought Implies Can, contrapositive of
Christianity 1, 32–33, 61–62, 64, 79; *see also* gods/God
collectives 3, 14
compatibilism 33–34, 80–81, 95
compulsion 34, 82–85; *see also* addiction
consequentialism 43–45, 57, 66; *see also* utilitarianism
control 13, 33, 35
conversational implicature 8–9, 37, 39–40, 76
Copp, David 43–44, 46–47, 59–60, 64–65
cost, personal 44–45, 47, 77, 92–94
Cullity, Garrett 49, 54

culpable ignorance 69, 80–81, 86
culpable inability 17, 24, 53–54

Darrow, Clarence 80–81
Darwall, Stephen 27
de la Cruz, Sor Juana Inés 2
death penalty 80–81
deliberation 1, 40, 59, 70, 98
demandingness 42–49, 57, 70, 86–87, 92–95, 97–98
deontic logic 7–8, 10, 31
derivative oughts *see* ought, derivative
determinism 33–34, 41, 79–85, 95
diachronic Ought Implies Can 16–18, 24, 28, 41
difficulty 44–45, 47, 51, 73, 77, 84, 92–94
disability 81–83
divine command theory *see* gods/God

egalitarianism 52; luck, 91; *see also* fairness, as egalitarian
emotions *see* mental states
entailment 7–9, 20, 27, 37, 41; *see also* implication
epistemically bounded principles 4, 56–57, 65–66, 69, 75
equality 47–49, 87–92; *see also* fairness, as egalitarian
ethics of care 2, 74–75
excuses 27, 34, 58
experimental philosophy 26–27, 82–83

fairness 2, 22, 25, 42–58, 60, 68–70, 75, 81, 87–91, 94–95, 97–99; as egalitarian 52–53, 55; and the law 85–87; *see also* Agential Fairness principle; Institutional Fairness principle; Unfair Demands; Interpersonal Fairness principle; Pretheoretical Fairness principle
familial obligations *see* obligation, familial
feasibility 13, 20, 92–96
feminism 2
Frankfurt cases 35–36, 53, 74, 92
Frankfurt, Harry 21, 35–36, 41
free will 13, 33–34, 79–81
Frege, Gottlob 8

gay rights 87–90
gender 90–92, 95

general obligations *see* obligation, general
gods/God 1, 24, 32–33, 43, 47, 60–62, 64, 76, 79, 88, 95
Graham, Peter 56
guilt 27, 31, 76, 94; legal notion of 80–81, 85–87

Heuer, Ulrike 64
homosexuality *see* sexual orientation
Hume, David 25–26
hypocrisy 51, 53

ill will 53, 58, 86–87, 91–92
implication 3, 7–9
inability *see* ability; culpable inability; disability
inference to the best explanation 66, 68; as motivation for OIC 2, 42, 66–68, 70, 75, 97
Institutional Fairness principle 47–49, 55
institutions 14, 47–49, 71, 74, 87, 91–94; *see also* laws; Institutional Fairness principle
intention 32–33, 35, 53–54, 69–70, 72, 80–81, 83–87, 91, 97
Interpersonal Fairness principle 50–55, 94
is-ought gap 25–26

Jay, Christopher 62
justice 30, 49, 71, 73, 87, 91

Kant, Immanuel 1, 19, 22–23, 25–26
Kühler, Michael 45

laws 26, 29, 47–49, 53, 57, 58, 71, 73, 78, 85–87, 91, 93, 95, 98
laws of nature *see* possibility, nomological
Leopold and Loeb 80–81

Manson, Neil 92
Marx, Karl 1
Mengzi 2
mens rea 85–86
mental states 14–15, 23, 31–33, 56, 83, 95; *see also* action, complex; intention

Index 109

metatheoretical principles 17–18; *see also* Ought Implies Can, as metatheoretical principle
mètre des Archives 48
modal logic 7–8, 10, 31
Moore, Michael 43
moral dilemmas 29–31, 36–37, 41, 43, 72–74, 77, 85
moral obligation 2, 5–6, 13–14, 18, 26–33, 51, 54, 56–57, 64, 67, 69, 74, 80; and disability 82; and the law 95; and non-natural obligation 80; and ought *see* ought, and obligation; and political institutions 92; *see also* obligation
Moral Ought Implies Can (Moral OIC) 17–18, 41, 50, 54, 58, 60, 70, 76, 85–87, 94, 95; *see also* Unfair Demands principle
moral realism 41
moral responsibility 33–37, 41, 53, 68–69, 79–81, 86, 98; *see also* blameworthiness
moral theory 17–18, 43–50, 55–57, 63, 77; *see also* normative ethics
must 6

Nagel, Thomas 2
natural duties 71
Natural Ought Principle 71–76, 78; *see also* ought, natural
No Absurd Oughts principle 67, 70; *see also* inference to the best explanation, as motivation for OIC
Noddings, Nel 2
Non-Natural Ought Principle 71–76; *see also* ought, non-natural
normative ethics 73–76, 83, 98–99
normativity 3–4, 22–26

obligation 24; institutional 71, 93–95; familial 30, 71–74, 77; general 77; legal 26, 85, 95, *see also* laws; moral *see* moral obligation; natural *see* ought, natural; non-natural *see* ought, non-natural; positional 71; promissory *see* promises; remote 15–17; role 28–29, 31, 71–72; special 30, 71, 74
omissions 15, 35–37
O'Neill, Onora 92

opportunity 11–12, 18, 20, 34, 72–74
ought 3–6; all-things-considered 5–6, 18–19, 23–24, 70–76; derivative 24, 64–65; epistemic 3–5; ideal 3–4, 19, 23; legal 4–5, 26; moral 3–6, 23–24, 69–76; natural 71–76, 80, 82–85, 95; non-natural 71–76, 79, 80, 83–84, 93, 95; normative 3–4, 6, 19, 25; objective 4, 6, 56; and obligation 5–6, 18–19, 71–72; ought to be 4, 14–15, 31, 33, 88–89; practical 5, 70; predictive 3–4, 23; *prima facie* 19–20; pro tanto 5–6, 30; prudential 3–5, 73; subjective 4, 23, 56; *ultima facie see* all-things-considered
Ought Implies Can: as analytic truth 7–9, 18; as conceptual truth 7–9, 18, 41; as conditional 7–8; as diachronic 16–18; as empirical claim 8; as metatheoretical principle 8, 17–18, 41; as moral claim 8, 17–18, 41, 49–54, 60, 85, 97, *see also* Moral Ought Implies Can; as pragmatic 8, 41, 60–61, 97; as rule of inference 7–8; as synchronic 16–18, 21; error theory of 76; how to temporally index 3, 15–18; counterexamples to 25–37; contrapositive of 25–26, 38–40; motivations for adopting 22, 42–68, 97–99; motivations for denying 22–25, 97–99; revisionism about 76; standard version of 18–19
Ought Implies Can Avoid (OICA) 13–14, 21, 60, 76
Ought Implies Could Have *see* diachronic Ought Implies Can
Ought Implies Evidence (OIE) 56–57; *see also* epistemically bounded principles
Ought Implies Feasible 92–95
overridingness 5–6, 29–31

parsimony 18, 23–24, 75
Pelagius 1
pointlessness 60–63, 76
policy 78, 90–94, 98
political philosophy 71, 92
politics 73, 87–93, 98

positional obligations *see* obligation, positional
possibility 10–11: circumstantial 11; logical 10, 73; metaphysical 10, 20, 73; nomological 10, 20, 73; physical 10; psychological 11; practical 11
pragmatics 8–9, 37–41, 98
presupposition 8–9, 37–39, 63, 76; pragmatic 8, 63; semantic 8, 63
Pretheoretical Fairness principle 54–57, 68, 70, 75
Principle of Alternate Possibilities 21, 34–37, 41, 53, 74, 83, 88, 92
promises 27–31, 64, 72, 74; examples using 4–6, 13, 15, 26–31, 53–54, 72, 80, 82
prudence 3, 5, 73
public policy *see* policy
punishment 43, 51, 58, 69–70, 78–81, 85–92, 94–95

race 90–92
racism 90–92
Rational Intending principle 69–70, 75; *see also* intention
rationality 5, 13–14, 60, 69–70, 72–73, 75–76, 97; *see also* Rational Intending principle
reasons 3, 5–6, 18, 22, 28, 77; "crazy" 77; *see also* No Absurd Oughts principle
Reasons Imply Can 5, 28
reflective equilibrium 37
remote obligations *see* obligation, remote

role obligations *see* obligation, role
Russell, Bertrand 8

Saka, Paul 61
science 55, 68, 80, 88–89, 92–93; *see also* theory building
sexism 90–92
sexual orientation 87–90
should 6
Sidgwick, Henry 2
Simmons, A. John 71
Singer, Peter 2
special obligations *see* obligation, special
speech acts 28, 62–63, 79
Statman, Daniel 43
Stern, Robert 43, 61–62
Strawson, Peter 8
supererogation 5, 64
synchronic Ought Implies Can 16–18, 21, 24, 28, 41

theory building 18, 47–50, 54–55, 68, 93
trying 11–13, 20, 32, 92

Unfair Demands principle 50–54, 70, 87, 94
utilitarianism 66, 74–75; *see also* consequentialism

Vranas, Peter 45

Williams, Bernard 43

For Product Safety Concerns and Information please contact our EU representative GPSR@taylorandfrancis.com
Taylor & Francis Verlag GmbH, Kaufingerstraße 24, 80331 München, Germany